westermann

FiNALE
Prüfungstraining

2025
Berlin / Brandenburg

Mittlerer Schulabschluss /
Erweiterte Berufsbildungsreife

Englisch

Liebe Schülerin, lieber Schüler,

sobald die Original-Prüfungsaufgaben zur Veröffentlichung freigegeben sind, können sie unter **www.finaleonline.de** zusammen mit ausführlichen Lösungen kostenlos heruntergeladen werden. Gib dazu einfach diesen Code ein:

EN8v2Fw

Einfach mal reinschauen: www.finaleonline.de

Autorinnen: Katrin Frost
sowie Elke Dreyer

© 2024 Westermann Lernwelten GmbH, Georg-Westermann-Allee 66, 38104 Braunschweig
www.westermann.de

Druck A[1] / Jahr 2024
Alle Drucke der Serie A sind im Unterricht parallel verwendbar.

Redaktion: Federlese GbR – Christina & Boris Kühne, Grevenbroich
Kontakt: finale@westermanngruppe.de
Layout: LIO Design GmbH, Braunschweig
Umschlaggestaltung: Janssen Kahlert Design & Kommunikation GmbH, Hannover
Umschlagfoto: stock.adobe.com, Dublin, Cookie Studio; iStockphoto.com, Calgary, Jane_Kelly
Druck und Bindung: Westermann Druck GmbH, Georg-Westermann-Allee 66, 38104 Braunschweig

ISBN 978-3-07-**172587**-4

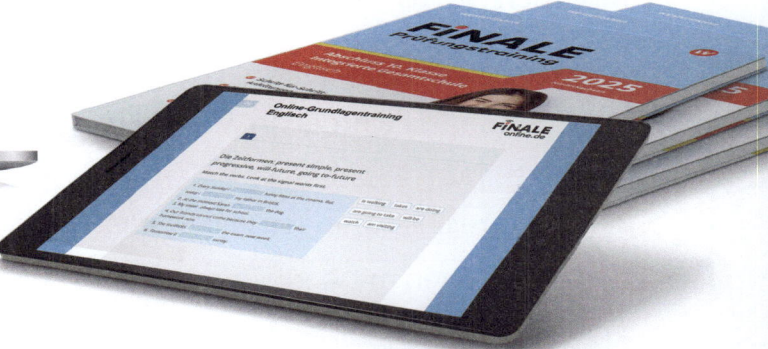

FiNALE Prüfungstraining

Grundlagentraining Englisch

Das FiNALE Grundlagentraining ist die optimale Ergänzung zu diesem Arbeitsbuch. Es bietet eine große Auswahl an Materialien, mit deren Hilfe du prüfungsrelevantes Grundlagenwissen auffrischen und aktiv trainieren kannst.

Folgende Inhalte werden in diesem Band behandelt:

- umfangreiche Übungen zur Grammatik
- Hörverstehen mit Audiodateien
- Leseverstehen
- Schreiben
- Sprachmittlung (Mediation)
- Sprechen
- die wichtigsten Operatoren im Fach Englisch

FiNALE Prüfungstraining
Grundlagentraining Englisch
ISBN 978-3-7426-1891-7
13,95 €

FiNALE Grundlagentraining gibt es auch für die Fächer Deutsch und Mathematik.

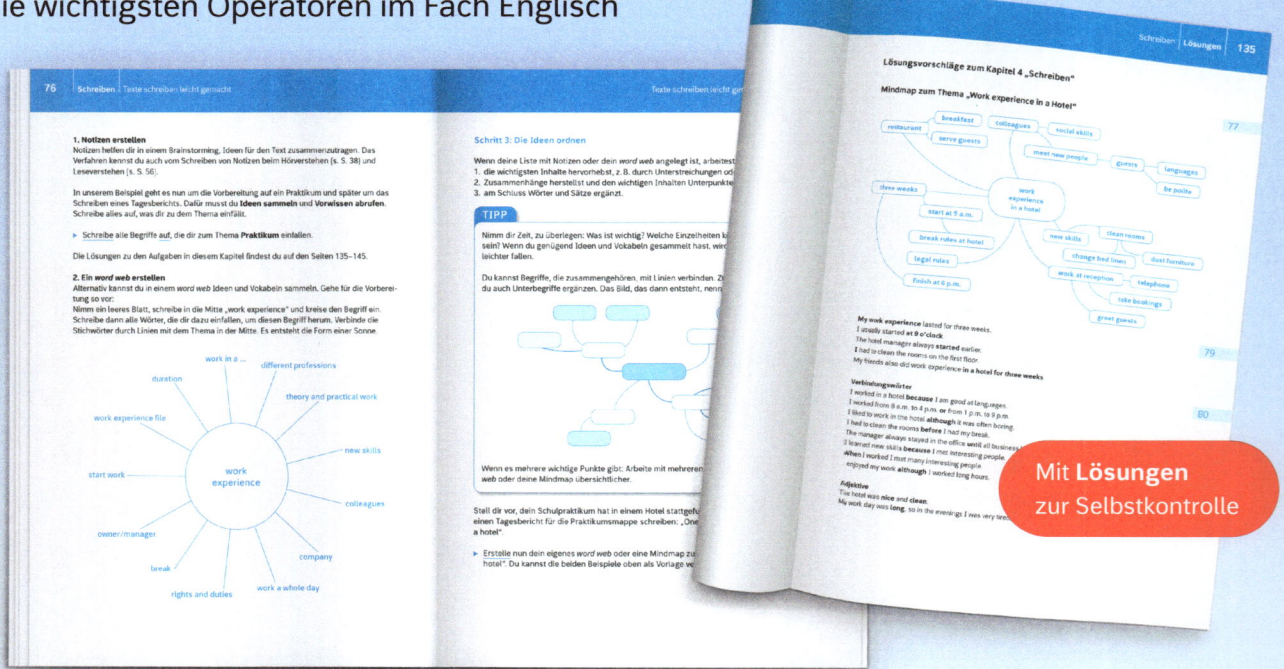

Was erwartet dich in diesem Buch?

In einigen Wochen oder Monaten wirst du in Berlin oder Brandenburg die Abschlussprüfung im Fach Englisch ablegen. Um dir die Aufregung vor diesen bevorstehenden schriftlichen und mündlichen Tests zu nehmen und dich mit den Prüfungsanforderungen und Aufgabenformaten vertraut zu machen, haben wir Beispielaufgaben und Tipps zur gezielten Vorbereitung zusammengestellt. Alle Beispielprüfungen orientieren sich inhaltlich und sprachlich an den Berliner Originalprüfungen der letzten Jahre. Wenn du dieses Buch also schrittweise durcharbeitest, Tipps und Tricks verinnerlichst und erfolgreich anwendest, wirst du den Abschlussprüfungen ruhig und entspannt entgegensehen.

Teil A widmet sich der *schriftlichen* Abschlussprüfung. In diesem Abschnitt erhältst du vorbereitende Informationen
1. zum organisatorischen Ablauf und den einzelnen Prüfungsteilen sowie
2. zu den Aufgabenformaten der Prüfungsschwerpunkte Hören, Lesen, Schreiben und Mediation (Berlin) beziehungsweise für die Überprüfung des Hörverstehens und Leseverstehens (Brandenburg).
In kleinen Schritten wirst du an die Aufgabentypen herangeführt und durch Lösungshilfen und geeignete Strategien bei der erfolgreichen Bewältigung der Tests gezielt unterstützt.

Im zweiten Teilabschnitt findest du drei angeleitete Prüfungsbeispiele, die von den Aufgabenstellungen und dem Schwierigkeitsgrad Originalprüfungen entsprechen. Hier kannst du deine Kenntnisse in aller Ruhe und ohne Stress überprüfen. Zu deiner Unterstützung findest du Lösungshilfen und Tipps, die dir die spätere selbstständige Vorgehensweise erleichtern. Der vierte Test ist die Originalprüfung Berlin aus dem Jahr 2023. Die Originalprüfung für das Jahr 2024 bekommst du im Internet, sobald sie geschrieben und zur Veröffentlichung freigegeben ist. Sie ist dann zu finden unter www.finaleonline.de und kann mit dem Code von Seite 4 heruntergeladen werden.

Hast du vielleicht noch Lücken aus den vorherigen Schuljahren? Dann empfehlen wir dir das FiNALE Grundlagentraining Englisch (ISBN 978-3-7426-1891-7). Es bietet prüfungsrelevantes Grundlagenwissen zum Nachschlagen und Üben. Ergänzend dazu findest du unter www.finaleonline.de/grundlagentraining ein kostenloses Online-Training bestehend aus interaktiven Übungsaufgaben und zahlreichen Arbeitsblättern zum Ausdrucken.

In **Teil B** erhältst du Informationen zur *mündlichen* Prüfung. Auch hier widmet sich der erste Abschnitt
1. dem organisatorischen Ablauf und
2. den Prüfungsthemen bzw. -formaten.
Darüber hinaus haben wir dir auch hier eine Sammlung von Strategien und Hilfen zur effektiven Prüfungsvorbereitung zusammengestellt. Du findest zahlreiche Redewendungen sowie Tipps und Tricks, die dir helfen, im mündlichen Prüfungsgespräch erfolgreich zu bestehen.

Alle Übungen, zu denen es Audio-Dateien gibt, erkennst du an diesem Symbol 🎧. Um die Audio-Dateien anzuhören, gib auf der Internetseite www.finaleonline.de den Code von Seite 4 ein.
Dem Buch beigelegt ist natürlich ein Lösungsheft.

Wir sind uns sicher, dass du dich nach der Bearbeitung dieses Buches für das „Finale" gewappnet fühlst, und wünschen dir für die Prüfung viel Erfolg.

Das Autorenteam

Teil A Die schriftliche Prüfung

A 1 Vorbereitung: Let's get ready for the test!

A 1.1 Was wird in der schriftlichen Prüfung erwartet?

Die zentrale Abschlussprüfung im Fach Englisch ist in Berlin und Brandenburg eine **kombinierte** Prüfung zur erweiterten Berufsbildungsreife (eBBR) und zum mittleren Schulabschluss (MSA). Das bietet dir die Chance, entweder die Anforderungen für die eBBR oder für den MSA zu erfüllen. Dabei entscheidet die Anzahl der erreichten Punkte darüber, welchen der beiden Schulabschlüsse du erzielt hast.

Die schriftliche Prüfung in Berlin enthält Aufgaben zum Hör- und Leseverstehen, zum Schreiben und zur Sprachmittlung. Damit unterscheidet sie sich sicher nicht sehr von Klassenarbeiten, mit denen du schon vertraut bist.

> **INFO** Prüfung in Brandenburg
>
> Die zentrale schriftliche Abschlussprüfung im Land Brandenburg ist wie auch die Berliner Prüfung eine kombinierte Prüfung zur erweiterten Berufsbildungsreife (EBR) und zur Fachoberschulreife (FOR). Die erzielte Gesamtpunktzahl entscheidet darüber, welcher der beiden Schulabschlüsse erreicht wird.
>
> In ihrer schriftlichen Prüfung bearbeiten Schülerinnen und Schüler im Land Brandenburg ausschließlich Aufgaben zur Überprüfung des Hör- und Leseverstehens. Diese Prüfung entspricht den Teilen Hörverstehen und Leseverstehen der schriftlichen Prüfung des Landes Berlin. Detaillierte Informationen zum auch in Brandenburg durchgeführten Teil findest du unter A 1.2, A 1.4 und A 1.5.
>
> Alle weiteren Informationen zum Aufbau und Ablauf der schriftlichen Abschlussprüfung beziehen sich daher auf die Prüfung des Landes Berlin.

A 1.2 Zum Aufbau der schriftlichen Prüfung

Die schriftliche Prüfungsarbeit besteht in Berlin aus zwei Teilen, in denen unterschiedliche Fertigkeiten überprüft werden:

Teil I: Hörverstehen

Teil II: Leseverstehen und Schreiben

Im **ersten Teil** der Prüfung wird das Hörverstehen überprüft. Dazu werden dir vier verschiedene Hörtexte vorgespielt. Hierbei sticht vor allem der vierte Hörtext durch Länge und Anspruch hervor. Aufgaben mit einem erhöhten Anforderungsniveau sind durch Sternchen (*) gekennzeichnet.

Zu jedem Hörtext erhältst du unterschiedliche Aufgaben, z. B. das Zuordnen von Bildern zu (Lautsprecher-) Ansagen oder die Auswahl der korrekten Lösung aus mehreren Antwortmöglichkeiten (Multiple Choice). Diese Aufgabenarten sind dir sicherlich nicht neu. **Aber Vorsicht:** Lass dich nicht täuschen! Oft sind die Antwortmöglichkeiten derart ähnlich, dass man leicht etwas Falsches ankreuzt. Es gilt, genau hinzuhören und die Aufgabenstellung und Antwortmöglichkeiten in Ruhe zu bedenken.

Im **zweiten Teil** der Prüfung werden deine Fertigkeiten im Lesen und Schreiben getestet. Du erhältst einen zweiten Aufgabenbogen, den du selbstständig und in deinem individuellen Tempo bearbeiten kannst.

Das **Leseverstehen** wird anhand drei unterschiedlicher Leseaufgaben überprüft. In der Regel wird hier getestet, ob und inwieweit du in der Lage bist, unterschiedlich langen Texten beziehungsweise Textsorten Informationen zu entnehmen. Das Textangebot reicht von Hinweisschildern bis hin zu längeren Zeitungsartikeln. Zu jedem Lesetext bekommst du Aufgaben, zu denen du wiederum die richtigen Lösungen auf dem Aufgabenbogen angeben sollst. Das sind in der Regel Auswahl-(Multiple Choice) und Zuordnungsaufgaben (*matching*). Auch hier gilt: Nimm dir Zeit und lies die Aufgabe und die Antwortmöglichkeiten **genau** durch! Ein voreiliges Vorgehen führt auch hier schnell zu Fehlentscheidungen.

Bei der **ersten Schreibaufgabe** sollst du in der Regel einen Beitrag in einem Online-Chat schreiben. Du sollst einen kurzen Text zu einem Foto schreiben, das du gepostet hast. Dabei wird dir ein Foto vorgegeben, zu dem Freunde Fragen gestellt haben. Diese Fragen sollst du nun beantworten. Tipps und Hinweise dazu findest du im Kapitel 1.6 „Schreiben".

In der **zweiten Schreibaufgabe** wird dir beispielsweise ein Beitrag eines gleichaltrigen Teenagers aus einem Onlineforum präsentiert, auf den du angemessen antworten sollst. Es wird von dir erwartet, dass du gestellte Fragen und Aufforderungen ausführlich und natürlich sprachlich korrekt beantwortest.

Die **dritte Schreibaufgabe** überprüft deine Fähigkeit, Informationen aus deutschen Texten sinngemäß und zweckgebunden ins Englische zu übertragen (Mediation). Dabei kann es zum Beispiel um Freizeitaktivitäten oder Ideen für Projektwochen gehen. Wichtig ist es, zu beachten, dass du Inhalte nicht wörtlich übersetzen, sondern sinngemäß übertragen sollst. Nützliche Tipps und Strategien zur Umschreibung von Wörtern und Wortgruppen findest du im Kapitel 1.7 „Mediation".

INFO zu den Schreibaufgaben

Zur Überprüfung deiner Schreibfertigkeit werden dir in der Regel drei Aufgaben gestellt:

1. Schreiben eines Beitrags in einem Online-Chatroom
2. Antwort auf einen Online-Forumsbeitrag
3. sinngemäßes Übertragen von Informationen ins Englische.

A 1.3 Weitere Hinweise und Informationen zur schriftlichen Prüfung

1. In den Aufgaben zur Überprüfung des Hör- und Leseverstehens erhältst du für jede richtige Antwort einen Punkt.
2. Zur Bearbeitung aller Prüfungsaufgaben stehen dir **insgesamt 150 Minuten** zur Verfügung: 45 Minuten für den Hörverstehensteil (Teil I) und 105 Minuten für den Leseverstehensteil (Teil II).
3. Die Benutzung eines Wörterbuches oder anderer Hilfsmittel ist **nicht gestattet**.
4. Die Aufsicht führende Lehrkraft beantwortet während der Prüfung keine fachlichen Fragen. Du musst dir die Aufgaben also immer ganz genau durchlesen.

A 1.4 Hören

Im Hörverstehensteil der Prüfung kannst du zeigen, inwiefern du in der Lage bist, aus unterschiedlich langen und komplexen Hörtexten detaillierte bzw. globale Informationen zu entnehmen. Das können Lautsprecherdurchsagen, Sprachnachrichten, Radiospots, Diskussionen oder Gespräche sein, wie sie dir in englischsprachigen Ländern tatsächlich begegnen können. Dabei musst du dich je nach Sprechsituation und/oder Herkunft der Sprechenden auf verschiedene Hintergrundgeräusche, variierende Sprechgeschwindigkeiten und auch unterschiedliche Akzente der englischen Sprache einstellen. Das erfordert viel Konzentration, weshalb die Überprüfung des Hörverstehens in der Regel zu Beginn der Prüfung erfolgt.

TIPP Radiospots

Radiospots sind häufig extrem kurz und werden sehr schnell gesprochen. Deshalb ist es wichtig, auf dir bekannte Schlüsselwörter (Nomen und Verben) zu achten. Sie geben dir oft Hinweise auf das Thema oder die Textaussage. Auch Hintergrundgeräusche verraten dir etwas über den Ort oder die Situation.

In den verschiedenen Aufgabenformaten werden drei Arten des Hörverstehens überprüft:

Globales Hörverstehen bedeutet, dass du den Hauptgedanken eines Hörtextes verstehst. Dazu musst du meist herausfinden, wer mit wem spricht, was die allgemeine Sprechsituation ist (z. B. auf dem Bahnhof, am Telefon usw.) und worum es allgemein geht. Einzelheiten sind dabei nicht so wichtig.

Durch **selektives Hörverständnis** beweist du, dass du die Antwort auf eine ganz bestimmte Frage heraushören kannst. Du versuchst also, ganz gezielt eine Information (einen Preis, eine Uhrzeit, eine Bahnsteignummer usw.) herauszuhören. Die anderen Informationen des Textes musst du dafür nicht vollständig verstehen. **Detailliertes Hörverstehen** ist wichtig, wenn du Einzelheiten und genauere Informationen oder Haltungen aus Gesprächen oder Berichten entnehmen sollst. Diese Art des Hörverstehens erfordert sicherlich die höchste Konzentration, da auf alles Gesagte geachtet werden muss.

INFO zu den Aufgabentypen

Zur Überprüfung des Hör- und Leseverstehens werden in der Regel folgende Arten von Aufgabentypen verwendet:

1. *Multiple choice* (= *Tick the correct answer.*)
2. *Note-taking* (= *Complete a table/grid using keywords.*)
3. *Matching* (= *Find the matching "partner(s)".*)

Welche Aufgabenformate erwarten dich beim Hören?

Insgesamt erwarten dich vier unterschiedliche Aufgabenteile, die wie folgt aussehen:

Im **ersten Hörverstehensteil** geht es darum, **detaillierte Fakten** aus Lautsprecheransagen oder anderen öffentlichen Durchsagen sowie Telefon- oder Voicemailnachrichten herauszuhören. Das können Uhrzeiten, Ortsangaben, Wettererscheinungen, Werbeprodukte oder ähnliche Informationen sein. Du erhältst zu jeder Frage vier Auswahlmöglichkeiten, die jeweils durch ein Bild unterlegt werden. Deine Aufgabe ist es, dich für das richtige Bild entscheiden.

AUFGABENBEISPIEL ZUM 1. HÖRVERSTEHENSTEIL

- You are going to hear four people reacting to pictures.
- Look at the pictures and then listen to each message.
- Decide which picture each speaker reacts to and put a tick in the right box.
- You can listen to the recording twice.

1. Which picture does the speaker react to?

A ☐ B ☐ C ☐ D ☐

Im **zweiten Hörverstehensteil** werden dir etwa vier **Radiospots** (z. B. Radiowerbungen) vorgespielt. Diese haben oft ein hohes Sprechtempo und sind zum Teil mit Musik oder anderen Geräuschen unterlegt. Deine Aufgabe ist hier, den Hauptgedanken des Spots zu erkennen. Dazu bekommst du in der Aufgabenstellung eine Liste von fünf bis sechs Slogans, die du dem jeweiligen Spot zuordnen musst, oder du bekommst pro Radiospot mehrere Antwortmöglichkeiten und musst dich für eine entscheiden.

AUFGABENBEISPIEL ZUM 2. HÖRVERSTEHENSTEIL

You are going to hear four radio spots.

- Read the six slogans below first.
- Choose the right slogan for each spot from the list and put a tick under the right letter (A–F) in the grid.
- There is only one slogan for each spot. Two slogans cannot be matched.
- You will hear the recording twice.

A) Become a paramedic and help others!

B) Experience a great festival at work!

C) Join Dr Howard and get fit!

D) Dare to dream big - write a book!

E) If you love it, repair it!

F) Think your town is boring? Go exploring!

Number	Radio Spot	Slogan					
		A	B	C	D	E	F
5	Radio Spot 1						
6	Radio Spot 2						
7	Radio Spot 3						
8*	Radio Spot 4						

Der **dritte Hörverstehensteil** überprüft im Anschluss deine Fähigkeit, wichtige Einzelinformationen aus längeren Monologen, Berichten verschiedener Sprecherinnen und Sprecher, Podcasts oder Gesprächen unter Freundinnen/Freunden herauszuhören und in Form von komprimierten Stichpunkten in eine Tabelle einzutragen. Dabei kann es sich oft um persönliche Erfahrungsberichte und Gespräche zu einem Thema handeln. Die Aufgabenstellung bzw. Tabelle gibt dir vor, zu welchen Aspekten dieses Themas du Informationen erfassen sollst. Unter Umständen sind bereits Teile der Tabelle exemplarisch ausgefüllt, und Zellen, zu deren Fragestellung im Hörtext keine Informationen vorkommen, sind durchgestrichen.

- You are going to hear three people talking about their favourite holiday.
- You can listen to the recording twice.
- Complete the table below. Use 1 to 5 words or numbers for each answer.

	Where did they go?	What did they do?	Best experience	Costs
	1	3	watching a falcon hunt	7
		4	5	8
	2		6	9

Im **vierten Hörverstehensteil** verfolgst du als Hörer/-in eine Talkshow oder Radiodiskussion zu einem alltags-relevanten Thema. Dabei diskutieren verschiedene Personen (manchmal moderiert), deren Argumente, aber auch Gefühle und Einstellungen du erkennen sollst. In der Aufgabenstellung bekommst du dazu verschiedene Antwortmöglichkeiten oder Aussagevarianten und musst die passenden heraushören und markieren.

- You are going to hear a radio programme about eco-friendly tourism.
- There are three speakers: Jenny O'Reilly (the host), Dr Louise Lehane (an environmental scientist), Tony Porter (a travel blog writer) and Hester Ingleman (a caller).
- Read the statements below first, then listen to the recording. Put a tick in the box next to the correct statement. Only one statement is correct.
- You can listen to the recording twice.

1. According to Dr Lehane, what is the first step in making one's travels more eco-friendly?	A	travelling by car instead of plane	☐
	B	travelling less	☐
	C	travelling to destinations closer to home	☐

Welche Strategien helfen dir beim Hörverstehen?

Alle Hörtexte der schriftlichen Prüfung werden dir zweimal vorgespielt. Du musst also nicht bereits nach dem ersten Hören alle Aufgaben und Fragen vollständig beantworten können.

Es gibt Strategien, die dir helfen, möglichst schnell und effektiv das Wichtigste zu erfassen. Das zweite Hören solltest du dann in jedem Fall dafür nutzen, deine Antworten genau zu überprüfen und wenn nötig zu ergänzen.

a) Vor dem Hören:

– Lies dir die Aufgabenstellung genau durch. Überlege, worum es im Hörtext gehen wird und was du schon über dieses Thema weißt. Denke darüber nach, welche englischen Wörter und Begriffe du zu diesem Thema erwarten würdest. Vielleicht begegnen dir diese ja dann wirklich im Text. Beachte, dass es manchmal mehrere Wörter für einen Begriff gibt.

– Finde aus der Aufgabenstellung genau heraus, welche Details oder Informationen du erfassen sollst.

– Schau dir vorgegebene Antwortmöglichkeiten in Ruhe an. Du kannst Schlüsselwörter auch vorab markieren, damit sie dir beim Hören gleich ins Auge fallen.

– Gibt es Aussagen, die dir von vornherein wenig sinnvoll erscheinen?

– Sprich dir vorgegebene Zahlen/Uhrzeiten stumm vor, dann fällt es dir vielleicht später leichter, sie herauszuhören.

– Konzentriere dich vor dem zweiten Hören auf die Aufgabenteile, bei denen du unsicher bist oder für die dir Informationen fehlen.

b) Beim Hören:

– Konzentriere dich auf die Aufgabe und bleibe möglichst entspannt.

– Du musst nicht jedes Detail verstehen. Falls du den Faden verlierst, gib nicht auf und setze später wieder ein.

– In der Regel sind die Aufgaben und Fragen in der Reihenfolge gestellt, wie die dazugehörigen Informationen im Hörtext vorkommen.

– Lass dich möglichst nicht von Hintergrundgeräuschen, Musik oder Akzentvarianten irritieren oder ablenken.

– Überprüfe beim zweiten Hören deine Auswahl/Antwort genau.

TIPP Hörverstehen langfristig trainieren

An der Anzahl und Vielfalt der Aufgabenformate erkennst du bereits, dass es sich lohnt, Ausdauer und Konzentrationsfähigkeit beim Hörverstehen gezielt und langfristig zu üben.

– Bestimmt haben viele deiner Lieblingsfilme und -serien ein englisches Original. Dann sieh dir regelmäßig eine Folge oder einen Film in englischer Sprache an. Dazu aktiviere am besten die englischen Untertitel. So kannst du Gehörtes auch parallel mitlesen. Beginne mit einem Film oder einer Serie, die du bereits kennst. Das macht den Einstieg leichter. Heutzutage bieten nicht nur DVDs, sondern auch viele andere Medienplattformen diese Sprachauswahloption.

– Hör bei deinen englischsprachigen Lieblingssongs doch mal genauer hin. Erkennst du, worum es in dem Lied geht? Zur Hilfe und Kontrolle kannst du manchmal eine Textoption nutzen oder den Songtext im Internet finden und beim Hören mitlesen.

– Verfolge die Nachrichten oder den Wetterbericht ab und zu auf Englisch. Englischsprachige Sender wie CNN oder BBC sind zum Beispiel über das Internet verfügbar. Dabei kann es hilfreich sein, wenn du dich vorher auf Deutsch über das Weltgeschehen/Wetter informierst und die Informationen dann vergleichst.

– Für viele deiner Lehrwerke (und auch für diesen Band) gibt es begleitende Hördateien auf CD oder im Netz. Nutze diese regelmäßig, um gezielt Höraufgaben zu üben oder Lesetexte mitzuhören.

– Das Internet bietet eine Vielzahl von Quellen für authentische Hörtexte. Du findest englischsprachige Vlogs, Radiosender, Podcasts und mehr zu den verschiedensten Themen. Wenn du dir etwas zum Hören auswählst, was dich interessiert, kannst du gleichzeitig deine Sprachkompetenz und dein Allgemeinwissen bereichern.

Wenn du auf diese Weise langfristig und regelmäßig trainierst, wirst du schnell merken, dass nicht nur dein Hörvermögen besser wird, sondern dass du auch deinen Wortschatz erweiterst und dein Gefühl für die englische Sprache und ihre Strukturen verbesserst.

A 1.5 Lesen

Bei den Leseverstehensaufgaben des MSA ist eine Auswahl an englischsprachigen Texten zu lesen und zu erfassen. Dabei wird von dir erwartet, dass du die Hauptaussage eines Lesetextes ohne die Hilfe eines Wörterbuches erschließt. Du musst aber auch in der Lage sein, detaillierte Fakten oder Einzelinformationen herauszulesen.

Insgesamt erwarten dich drei unterschiedliche Leseaufgaben.

Was erwartet dich?

Der **erste Leseverstehensteil** ist eine **Zuordnungsaufgabe**. Du erhältst Informationen zu fünf verschiedenen Personen, aufgrund derer du jeder Person aus einer Auswahl an Hobbys, Urlaubszielen, Büchern oder Ähnlichem zwei passende Items zuordnen musst.

Im **zweiten Leseverstehensteil** werden dir sechs **Kurzmitteilungen** (z. B. Reklame- oder Warnschilder, Verhaltensregeln, Hinweistafeln) präsentiert. Deine Aufgabe besteht darin, die Kernaussage dieser Mitteilungen zu erfassen.

Im **dritten Leseverstehensteil** erwartet dich ein längerer Artikel zu einem aktuellen Thema aus dem Bereich Kultur und Freizeit. Dieser Text handelt z. B. von berühmten Persönlichkeiten und ihren Aktivitäten oder gibt Hintergrundinformationen zu aktuellen Hobbys. Im Multiple-Choice-Verfahren musst du hier nachweisen, dass du sowohl die Kernaussage als auch detaillierte Textinformationen genau verstanden hast.

Lesetechniken kennen

In allen Prüfungsteilen zum Lesen sind folgende zwei **Lesetechniken** wichtig:

1. Das *skimming*: Diese Technik wendest du an, wenn du einen Text schnell überfliegst, um dir einen ersten **Überblick** darüber zu verschaffen, worum es überhaupt geht.
2. Das *scanning*: Diese Technik nutzt du, wenn du in einem Text nach **bestimmten Informationen** suchst, um Textverständnisfragen konkret zu beantworten.

Die Anwendung beider Techniken kannst du natürlich üben. Wenn du die folgenden Tipps und Tricks verinnerlichst, wirst du die Prüfungsaufgaben sicher wesentlich ruhiger und erfolgreicher in Angriff nehmen können.

Lesetechniken anwenden

Skimming – das „überfliegende" Lesen:

1. Schau dir zuerst die **Überschrift** an. Sie verrät dir oft schon, worum es in dem Text geht.
2. Der **erste** und der **letzte Satz** (eines Textabschnittes) sind häufig wesentlich für das inhaltliche Textverständnis.
3. Ist der Text in Abschnitte gegliedert? Jeder Abschnitt widmet sich in der Regel **einem Aspekt** des Themas (z. B. Kindheit, Karrierebeginn, heutiges Leben eines Stars) und hilft dir so, dich zu orientieren.

TIPP Lesen

– Lass dich beim Lesen nicht von unbekannten Wörtern demotivieren. Nicht jedes Wort oder Detail ist für die Lösung von Bedeutung.
– Lass Fragen, auf die du nicht sofort eine Antwort findest, zunächst ruhen. Markiere sie und beantworte sie nach Erledigung aller anderen Aufgaben.

Scanning – das „suchende" Lesen:
Du suchst gezielt nach Informationen, die dir helfen, konkrete Leseverständnisfragen zu beantworten (z. B. das Alter, Hobbys, Einstellungen oder gemeinnützige Aktivitäten einer Person). Dabei ist es oft nicht notwendig und eher zeitraubend, jeden einzelnen Satz ganz genau zu lesen.

1. Überfliege (*skimming*) den Text zunächst. Markiere **Schlüsselwörter** (Nomen, Verben, Jahreszahlen usw.) im Text (z. B. *years old, likes, hobbies, free time* oder *charity*), die dir später helfen, konkrete Textaussagen wiederzufinden.
2. Texte sind oft in Sinnabschnitte gegliedert. Teile sie farbig oder durch Bleistiftstriche voneinander ab.
3. Konzentriere dich ausschließlich auf diese markierten Textteile und finde Schlüsselwörter, die dir helfen, die Frage zu beantworten.

Du musst davon ausgehen, dass du beim ersten Überfliegen der Texte auf eine Vielzahl unbekannter Wörter und Wendungen stößt. Da es sich um authentische Texte, d. h. Originaltexte aus dem englischsprachigen Raum handelt, ist das auch normal und keineswegs ein Grund zur Panik. Wichtig ist, dass du Strategien kennst und anwendest, die dir helfen, strukturiert an die Leseaufgaben heranzugehen und die geforderten Informationen gezielt zu finden. Die folgende Vorgehensweise beziehungsweise **Schrittfolge** soll dich dabei unterstützen.

Schritt 1: Bereite dich auf das Lesen vor.
– Lege Materialien zum Markieren und Hervorheben von Textinformationen bereit. Das können farbige Textmarker, Buntstifte und ein Lineal sein.
– Gibt es Bilder oder eine Überschrift, die dir vielleicht schon eine Idee vom Textinhalt geben?
– Lies nun die Aufgabenstellung genau durch. Worauf musst du dich beim Lesen wirklich konzentrieren? Markiere bereits in der Aufgabenstellung wichtige Wörter und/oder Hinweise.
– Schaue anschließend die Lösungsvarianten an. Sie geben dir wichtige Hinweise auf die Textaussage bzw. einzelne wichtige Details, auf die du beim Lesen gezielt achten musst.

Schritt 2: Lies den Text aktiv.
– Lies den gesamten Text zunächst einmal zügig durch. So bekommst du einen guten Überblick, worum es überhaupt geht.
– Lies den Text jetzt unter Beachtung der Aufgabenstellung. Markiere nun wichtige Schlüsselwörter oder Wortgruppen, die für die Beantwortung der Fragen wesentlich sind. Nutze dabei verschiedene Farben für verschiedene Aspekte.

Mit unbekannten Wörtern umgehen
Beim Lesen englischsprachiger Texte werden dir immer wieder Wörter und Wendungen begegnen, die du nicht kennst. Das geht dir sicher auch bei der Lektüre einer deutschen Zeitung so, und es ist kein Anlass zur Besorgnis. Um einen Text im Gesamtzusammenhang zu verstehen, muss man nicht jedes einzelne Wort kennen. Wenn dir ein bestimmtes Wort allerdings wesentlich für das Textverständnis erscheint, können dir folgende Tipps zur Bedeutungserschließung vielleicht helfen:

1. Lässt sich die Bedeutung vielleicht aus dem Satzzusammenhang erschließen?

Beispiel: "Don't let your dog foul our streets and parks. Clean up!" Im Zusammenhang mit „dog", „streets" und anschließendem „clean" kann „foul" wahrscheinlich nur eine Bedeutung haben – das Beschmutzen der Straße durch den Hund in irgendeiner Form.

2. Erkennst du einen Wortstamm, von dem dieses Wort abgeleitet sein könnte?

Beispiele: „unrecognisable": „recognise" = erkennen, die Vorsilbe -un verneint etwas und die Nachsilbe -able entspricht dem Deutschen -bar (d. h. etwas ist machbar). „unrecognisable" könnte also bedeuten: nicht zu erkennen, nicht erkennbar bzw. unkenntlich.

„payment": „pay" = bezahlen; -ment = Substantivendung. Das Wort bedeutet demnach Bezahlung.

3. Lässt sich die Wortbedeutung aus der Muttersprache erschließen?

Beispiele: „phenomenon" = Phänomen; „spontaneous" = spontan, „debate" = Debatte bzw. debattieren

4. Ergibt sich eine Verbindung zu weiteren Fremdsprachen, die du vielleicht kennst?

Beispiele: „gouvernement" (frz. Regierung) = „government" (engl. Regierung); „violence" (frz. Gewalt) = „violence" (engl. Gewalt) ; „fortune" (frz. Glück) – „fortunately" (engl. zum Glück / glücklicherweise)

A 1.6 Schreiben

Die Schreibaufgaben der Prüfungen umfassen normalerweise verschiedene Textsorten und haben damit verbunden spezifische Anforderungen. Es wird zum Beispiel von dir erwartet, dass du in einem Onlineforum ein Bild kommentierst bzw. einen kurzen Text dazu schreibst oder auf einen Forumsbeitrag bzw. eine E-Mail zielgruppengerecht, fremdsprachlich korrekt und angemessen antwortest.

INFO zu den Schreibaufgaben

Zur Überprüfung deiner Schreibfertigkeit werden dir in der Regel drei Aufgaben gestellt:
1. Schreiben eines Beitrags in einem Onlineforum;
2. Antwort auf einen Forumsbeitrag;
3. sinngemäßes Übertragen von Informationen ins Englische.

Was erwartet dich?

In der **ersten Schreibaufgabe** werden dir Fragen zu einem von dir geposteten Foto gestellt. Dieses Foto hast du online veröffentlicht und musst dazu nun einen kurzen, sinnvollen Text schreiben.

In der **zweiten Schreibaufgabe** wird dir eine **E-Mail** beziehungsweise ein **Brief** einer/eines Gleichaltrigen präsentiert, den du zunächst lesen und verstehen musst. Deine Aufgabe besteht anschließend darin, auf die in der E-Mail gestellten Fragen ausführlich und sprachlich angemessen zu reagieren. In diesem Brief geht es in der Regel um ein kontroverses/streitbares Thema, z. B. den Umgang mit Taschengeld, unterhaltsame Freizeitaktivitäten oder sinnvolle Bemühungen gegen den Klimawandel.

Schreibtechniken kennen

a) Schreibaufgabe 1: Informationen zu einem Foto geben

Bevor du die Fragen des Chatmitglieds zu deinem Foto beantwortest, solltest du diese Schrittfolge einhalten:
1. Schau dir das Foto in Ruhe an. Stell dir vor, was passiert sein könnte. Lass deiner Fantasie freien Lauf!
2. Notiere dir nun die Fragen zum Foto auf einem Extrablatt.
3. Sammle Ideen und mache dir Notizen zu jeder Frage. So vergisst du nichts.
4. Die Notizen und Ideen helfen dir später, einen zusammenhängenden Text zu schreiben.

b) Schreibaufgabe 2: Auf einen Forumsbeitrag / eine E-Mail antworten

Vor dem Schreiben:

Auch hier sollst du auf Fragen aus einem Forumsbeitrag antworten. Deshalb ist es günstig, die Aufgabenstellung in den folgenden kleinen Schritten zu erledigen:

1. Lies den Forumsbeitrag zunächst sorgfältig durch.
2. Markiere das Thema. Häufig wird nur ein Thema behandelt.
3. Wichtig: Unterstreiche alle im Text gestellten Fragen. Denk daran, dass du in deiner Antwort möglichst alle Fragen ausführlich beantworten musst.
4. Nummeriere die Fragen und mache dir zunächst zu jeder Frage auf einem Extrablatt Notizen. Diese Notizen kannst du später ausformulieren.

Es ist immer sinnvoll, vor dem Schreiben Ideen zu sammeln. Diesen Schritt nennt man **Brainstorming**.

INFO zum Brainstorming

Beim Brainstorming schreibst du zuerst einmal alle spontanen Ideen und Einfälle zu einem Thema oder einer Fragestellung ungeordnet auf. Später sichtest und strukturierst du diese Ideen, als

– **Mindmap** (Das Thema wird dabei in die Mitte geschrieben, von dem Oberbegriffe oder Unterthemen abzweigen. An jeden Ast kannst du dann passende weitere Ideen schreiben.) oder als

– **Prioritätenliste** (Sichte deine Ideen oder Argumente und schreibe sie je nach persönlicher Gewichtung untereinander. Beginne mit der dir wichtigsten Idee.).

Gliedern – die Struktur guter Texte

Komplexere Texte, dazu gehören auch Briefe oder E-Mails, erkennt man an den folgenden **drei Abschnitten**. Nutze Absätze, um den Text zu strukturieren.

1. **Einleitung**
   (Bedanke dich für den Erhalt der E-Mail oder gehe knapp auf das allgemeine Thema ein, bevor du deine Antwort einleitest.)
2. **Hauptteil**
   (Hier schreibst du über dich, deine Erfahrungen bzw. deine Meinung. Du beantwortest dabei die Fragen, die dir gestellt wurden.)
3. **Schlussteil**
   (Fasse deine Ausführungen sinnvoll zusammen und/oder formuliere abschließende Fragen an dein Gegenüber. Verabschiede dich.)

INFO Redemittel – E-Mail/Brief (informell)

Anrede/Begrüßung: *Hello/Hi/Dear …*
Einleitungssatz: *Thank you (so much) for your email/letter. / Great to hear from you. / I'd love to …*
Abschluss/Verabschiedung: *Say hello to …(name) / Hope to hear from you soon. / Looking forward to hearing from you.*
Grußformel: *Yours/Love …*

Benutze beim Schreiben deines Textes keine Abkürzungen *(text language abbreviations)* wie „u" *(„you")*, „2" *(„to")* oder „coz" *(„because")*. Außerdem solltest du unbedingt auch Kurzformen wie „wanna" *(„want to")* oder „gonna" *(„going to")* vermeiden.

Nach dem Schreiben

Nimm dir nach Fertigstellung deines Textes unbedingt die Zeit, das Geschriebene noch einmal in Ruhe durchzulesen und zu korrigieren.

1. Ist der Text vollständig? Hast du alle erforderlichen Informationen eingefügt?
2. Findest du eventuell noch Rechtschreib- oder Grammatikfehler?

A 1.7 Mediation

Mediation bedeutet Sprachmittlung. Die Mediationsaufgabe in der schriftlichen Prüfungsarbeit testet deine Fähigkeit, wichtige Informationen aus deutschen Texten ins Englische zu übertragen. Das ist keine reine Übersetzungsaufgabe. Es geht vielmehr darum, für die Aufgabenstellung wesentliche Aspekte zu erkennen und dann sinngemäß ins Englische zu übertragen.

CHECKLISTE zum Verfassen eines Forumbeitrags / einer E-Mail

1. ☑ Ausgangstext lesen und Fragestellungen markieren/hervorheben
2. ☑ Brainstorming: Ideen sammeln und sortieren
3. ☑ Schreiben: Redemittel beachten, mit Absätzen strukturieren
4. ☑ Inhalt und Sprache überprüfen

Was erwartet dich?

Du erhältst zwei Ausgangstexte (z. B. Biografien, Erfahrungsberichte, Ausflugstipps etc.) in deutscher Sprache. Deine Aufgabe besteht darin, entsprechend der Aufgabenstellung einen Text für den gegebenen Anlass auszuwählen und Schlüsselinformationen in der Fremdsprache zu formulieren. Die Aufgabenstellung gibt dir Anhaltspunkte, welche und wie viele Informationen du zu welchem Zweck übertragen musst. Dabei sollst du eine E-Mail schreiben.

Um diese Aufgabe erfolgreich zu lösen, bietet es sich an, die folgende **Schrittfolge** einzuhalten:

1. Lies die Aufgabenstellung genau. Unterstreiche bzw. markiere die Informationen, die du konkret weitergeben musst.
2. Wenn nötig, mache dir zuerst Notizen auf einem Schmierzettel, bevor du die Aufgabe schriftlich ausarbeitest.

TIPPS zur Sprachmittlung

– Übersetze nicht Wort für Wort!
– Konzentriere dich auf das Wesentliche und lass unwichtige Einzelheiten weg.
– Formuliere kurze und einfache Sätze.
– Umschreibe Wörter, die du nicht kennst oder die dir (vor Aufregung) nicht einfallen.

Strategien zum Umschreiben von Wörtern

Es gibt verschiedene Möglichkeiten, Wörter zu umschreiben, die einem während der Prüfung nicht einfallen. Wenn du in diese Situation kommst, versuche es doch einmal so:

– Paraphrasiere das Wort, d. h., umschreibe es mit einem Wort, das dieselbe oder eine ähnliche Bedeutung hat. (z. B. „winzig" = *tiny* = **very small**)
– Versuche es mit dem Gegenteil. (z.B. „hell" = *bright* = **not dark**)
– Umschreibe das Wort mit einer Wortgruppe. (z. B. „Bahnsteig" = *platform* = **place where you get on a train**)
– Umschreibe mithilfe von Ober- bzw. Unterbegriffen. (z. B. „Besteck" = *cutlery* = **knives, forks and spoons**)
– Umschreibe den Begriff mit Relativsätzen, z. B.
  • *It is an animal that …*
  • *It is something you need/use for …*
  • *It is someone who …*
  • *It is a place where …*

A2 Angeleiteter Test 1

Teil I: Hörverstehen

Listening Part 1: Travelling by Train – Travel Announcements

 **Track 1**

TASKS

You are going to hear two announcements. There are two questions for each announcement.

- Look at the pictures and listen to the recording.
- Choose the correct picture and put a tick in the right box.
- You can listen to the recording twice.

Announcement One: At the station

1. Why is the train to Manchester Airport late?

  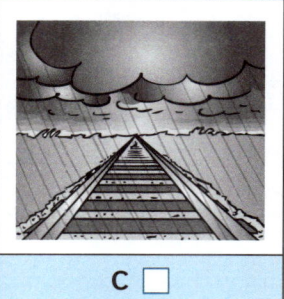 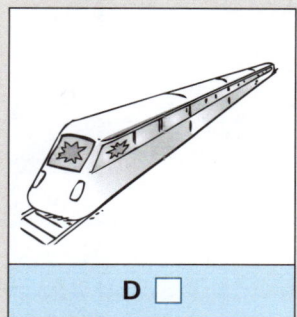

A ☒   B ☐   C ☐   D ☐

_____

_____

2. Which platform will the train leave from?

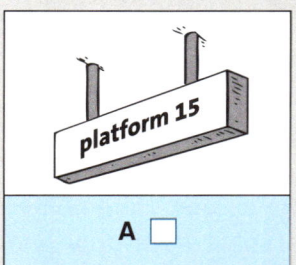 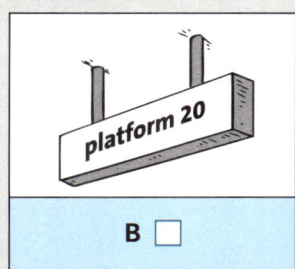 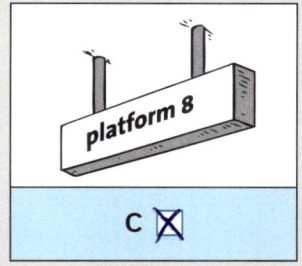 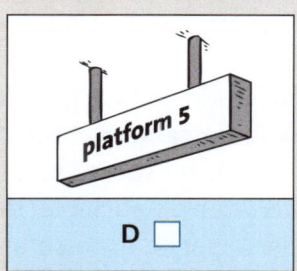

A ☐   B ☐   C ☒   D ☐

_____

Announcement Two: On the train

3. What can you get in the £ 4.99 meal deal?

A ⊠

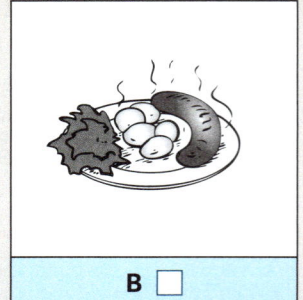

B ☐

C ⊠

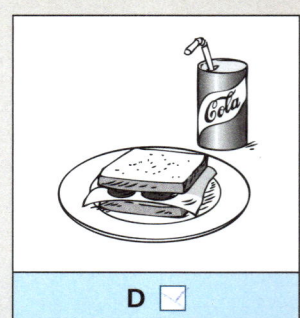

D ☑

_____

_____

4. Which is the Virgin train service to Manchester Piccadilly?

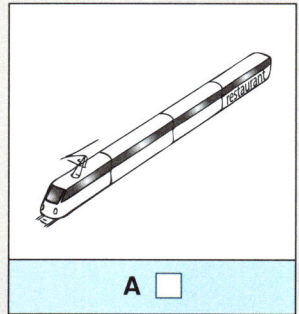

A ☐

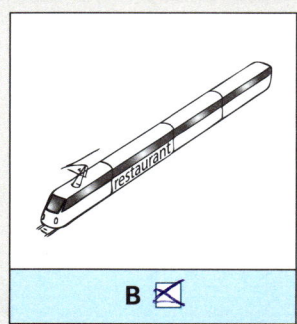

B ⊠

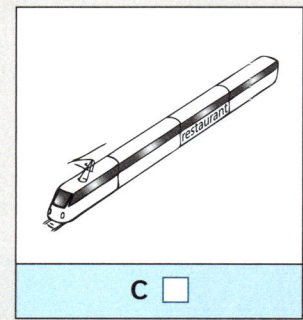

C ☐

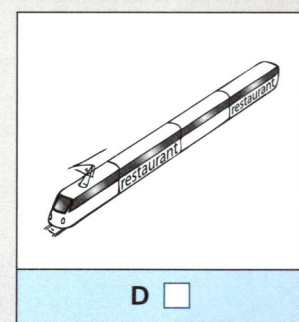

D ☐

_____

_____

LÖSUNGSHILFEN

Du erinnerst dich sicher an die Schritte, die man beim Hörverstehen beachten sollte (S. 13):
Lies dir die Aufgabenstellungen genau durch und schau dir die Bilder gut an.

Announcement 1: Die Aufgabenstellung verrät dir, dass du den Grund für die Verspätung eines **Zuges** erkennen sollst. Da das zweite Bild jedoch einen Flughafen zeigt, kannst du dieses Bild bereits ausschließen. Die Bilder 1 und 4 zeigen kaputte Dinge (Signal und Zugfenster). Achte hier also auf die Schlüsselwörter *signal* bzw. *windows*. Das dritte Bild erfordert die Wörter *rain* und / oder *clouds*.
Das Erkennen der korrekten Bahnsteignummer ist etwas einfacher. Sprich dir die vorgegebenen Zahlen vor dem Hören einfach noch einmal halblaut vor, sodass du den Klang bereits im Ohr hast.

Announcement 2: Die Überschrift „On the train" verrät dir, dass die folgende Ansage während der Zugfahrt erfolgt. Du sollst zuerst heraushören, welche Mahlzeit zu einem Sonderpreis angeboten wird. Die Bilder verraten dir auch hier die Schlüsselbegriffe, auf die du achten musst. Notiere sie dir vor dem Hören unter die Bilder: A. *pork, potatoes, salad*; B. *sausage, potatoes, salad*; C. *chicken, potatoes, salad, coke / drink* und D. *sandwich, coke / drink*.
In der letzten Teilaufgabe geht es um die Position des / der Zugrestaurants. Hilfreiche Schlüsselbegriffe könnten hier *first / last car, middle, front / mid position, (at the) front / back* sein.

Listening Part 2: Radio Ads

 **Track 2**

TASKS

You are going to hear four radio adverts.

- Read the statements below and listen to the recording.
- Tick the correct statement for each radio ad.
- You can listen to the recording twice.

5. (Ad 1)
This advert tells you …

A	how to buy tickets for Glastonbury Festival.	☐
B	how to get a first aid qualification.	☐
C	what kind of work you could do at Glastonbury Festival.	☒

6. (Ad 2)
This advert …

A	gives people the latest traffic news about highway construction work.	☐
B	wants people to buy environmentally friendly cars.	☒
C	wants people to team up and travel together in one car.	☐

7. (Ad 3)
This radio advert …

A	wants more people to ride a bicycle.	☐
B	tells people to wear a helmet when cycling.	☒
C	asks skateboarders to wear protective clothing.	☐

8. (Ad 4)
This radio spot is looking for people who …

A	give the money they normally earn in one hour to children in need.	☒
B	are prepared to spend one hour collecting money for children in need.	☐
C	want to do volunteer work in a children's home for one hour a week.	☐

LÖSUNGSHILFEN

a) Vor dem Hören:

Auch beim zweiten Aufgabenteil, dem Hörverstehen von Radiospots, solltest du dir zunächst die Aufgabenstellung und die Lösungsvorgaben genau durchlesen. Markiere bereits in den Lösungsvorgaben **Schlüsselwörter** (Nomen und Verben), die dir später als Signalwörter beim Textverständnis helfen.

Ad 1: Unterstreiche z. B.

A) *buy, tickets, festival;* B) *get, first aid qualification;* C) *kind of work, do, at festival*

b) Beim Hören:

Achte nun auf die **Hauptaussage** des Textes. Die unterstrichenen Schlüsselwörter helfen dir, wichtige Informationen „im Auge" zu behalten.

Achtung: In der Regel enthält jede Ankreuzmöglichkeit einen Aspekt, der in den Hörpassagen angesprochen wird. Nur eine passt aber genau. Lass dich also nicht irritieren und höre von Anfang bis Ende konzentriert zu.

Listening Part 3: The Summer Holidays

 **Track 3**

TASKS

- You are going to hear some friends talking about the summer holidays.
- You can listen to the recording twice.
- Complete the table below using keywords.

	holiday idea	0,5	reason why
David	9. start garden cleaning ✗		something you can be proud of ~~yourself~~
Tina	10. health and beauty day ✓		13. relaxing ✓
Michael	11. brunch ✓		14. diy and kreativ ✗
Becky	12. Yoga ✓		15. good for body ✓
Tom	volunteer work		16. great shape ✓
Karen	give your bedroom a new look		17. makes happy ✓

LÖSUNGSHILFEN

a) Vor dem Hören:

Lies zunächst die Überschrift und schau dir die Tabelle in Ruhe an: Es werden sich Freunde über ihre Pläne für die Sommerferiengestaltung unterhalten. Deine Aufgabe ist es, die Ideen und deren Begründung („reason why") stichpunktartig zu notieren.

b) Beim Hören:

Bewahre Ruhe. Höre konzentriert zu und notiere die Aussagen beziehungsweise Schlüsselwörter, die du verstehst. Wenn du etwas nicht sofort verstehst, ist das kein Problem. Du kannst den Text ein zweites Mal anhören.

c) Nach dem ersten Hören:

Markiere nun die Felder, auf die du beim zweiten Hören besonders achten musst. Konzentriere dich beim nächsten Durchgang vorrangig auf diese fehlenden Details.

*Listening Part 4: World Animal Day – Going Veggie?

 **Track 4**

TASKS

You are going to hear part of a radio talk about eating meat.
There are four people talking: a presenter, Amber, Dylan and Connor.

- Read the statements below and listen to the recording.
- Put a tick in the box next to the correct statement.
- In each task only one statement is correct.
- You can listen to the recording twice.

18. Of the three teenagers interviewed ...	A	everybody eats meat on a regular basis.	☐
	B	Amber and Dylan don't eat meat.	☐
	C	Amber is the only vegetarian.	☒ ✓

19. Amber stopped eating meat because ...	A	she thought eating vegetables was healthier.	☐
	B	her uncle had a vegetable farm and told her not to eat meat.	☒ ✗
	C	it felt wrong to her to play with the animals and then eat them.	☐ ✗

20. Amber's parents ...	A	were shocked that Amber wanted to be a vegetarian.	☐
	B	found her decision easy to live with.	☒ ✓
	C	had been vegetarians before.	☐

21. Connor thinks that ...	A	you should always eat salad and potatoes with your meat.	☒ ✗
	B	it's not healthy to be a vegetarian, especially as a child.	☐ ✗
	C	eating no meat at all would make him go crazy.	☐

22. Dylan ...	A	agrees with Connor that mass animal farming is necessary and natural.	☐
	B	thinks like Amber about the way animals are kept.	☒ ✓
	C	isn't interested in how animals are treated.	☐

23. Dylan has learned from a documentary that ...	A	turkeys are usually farmed very unnaturally to be fattened as quickly as possible.	☐
	B	eating turkey is unhealthy.	☒
	C	turkeys in the wild don't live for very long.	☐

24. According to Amber, giving up meat ...	A	can help fight climate change.	☐
	B	could reduce cases of heart disease by 50 %.	☒
	C	will lead to tastier vegetarian food options.	☐

25. Dylan thinks that ...	A	people should give up meat completely.	☒
	B	people shouldn't buy mass-produced meat.	☐
	C	it isn't necessary to kill animals.	☐

LÖSUNGSHILFEN

a) Vor dem Hören:

Schritt 1: Beachte zunächst einmal die Überschrift und die Aufgabenstellung. Sie verraten dir bereits, dass in der angekündigten Radiosendung das Thema „Tierrechte" beziehungsweise „fleischlose Ernährung" behandelt wird. Dazu werden drei Personen zu Wort kommen, d. h., es werden unterschiedliche Meinungen vertreten sein.

Schritt 2: Lies die Antworten genau durch und markiere Schlüsselbegriffe in den Lösungsvorgaben, die dir später als Signalwörter während des Hörens hilfreich sein können. Markiere zum Beispiel in Frage 19 die folgenden Begriffe:

A – *eating vegetables – healthier*
B – *uncle – vegetable farm – not eat meat*
C – *wrong to play – then eat*

Schritt 3: Überlege, ob es Antwortvorgaben gibt, die du bereits im Vorfeld ausschließen kannst bzw. für sehr unwahrscheinlich hältst. Kennzeichne sie. So kannst du zum Beispiel in Frage 18 die Antwort A bereits ignorieren, weil es sehr unwahrscheinlich ist, dass sich die drei Studiogäste auf dieselbe Art und Weise ernähren, da es dann wenig zu diskutieren gäbe.

b) Beim Hören: Nutze nun deine markierten Schlüsselbegriffe als Signalwörter. Sie helfen dir, dich auf das Wesentliche zu konzentrieren. Denk daran: Gib bei Verständnisschwierigkeiten nicht auf! Bleibe ruhig und versuche, mit dem Hören immer wieder neu anzuknüpfen.

Teil II: Leseverstehen/Schreiben

Reading Part 1: Out and About – Notices and Signs

- Read the text of each sign.
- Read the four statements next to it and decide which statement matches the sign.
- Tick the right statement. Only one of them is correct.

1.

SAY "NO" TO CRIME IN OUR COMMUNITY!

Lock your car at all times.
Don't leave your handbag, your money, your
mobile or other valuables in a parked car.
Report any suspicious activities and
emergencies to your local
police department under 0701011.

A	You can't park your car here.	☐
B	You don't need to lock your car if you park next to the police department.	☐
C	You should take things that are worth a lot with you.	☐
D	You must call 0701011 if you need more information.	☐

2.

At White Oak Hospital Park:

This hospital park is open to the public.
Please respect the park rules.
Take your litter home.
No alcoholic drinks allowed.
No skateboarding.
Park closes at dusk.

A	You can't drink beer in the park.	☐
B	You have to buy your drinks in the park.	☐
C	This park is only open to hospital patients.	☐
D	In summer the park is open 24 hours a day.	☐

3.

Dog fouling is litter!

**So don't let your dog foul streets,
parks or other people's gardens.
Clean up or pay up!
Minimum on-the-spot fine: £ 200**

A	You are not allowed to walk your dog in this park.	☐
B	It will cost a lot of money if you don't clean up after your dog.	☐
C	This sign asks you to use the bins for your litter.	☐
D	It costs £ 200 a year to use these gardens.	☐

4.

Do not chain your bicycle here.
Cars and lorries have to pass
through these gates at all times.
Any bikes chained to the gates will
be removed at the owner's expense.

A	You mustn't forget to lock your bicycle to the gate.	☐
B	You can't park your bike here.	☐
C	Only cars or lorries can park here.	☐
D	You can't park here today because the owner is moving.	☐

5.

Yosemite Park Sign:
Bear Warning
Proper food storage required.

Do not keep food in tents or
vehicles at night. Free bear-proof storage
boxes available at car park entrance.

A	This sign tells you how to feed the bears.	☐
B	You can buy proper food containers at the park reception.	☐
C	You must keep your food in special containers at night.	☐
D	There are no bears in this area.	☐

LÖSUNGSHILFEN

Lies zunächst die Aufgabe in Ruhe durch. Denk daran: Um sie erfolgreich zu lösen, musst du nicht jedes Wort verstehen!

Lies die Hinweisschilder und die dazugehörigen Antwortmöglichkeiten in Ruhe durch. Konzentriere dich auf Schlüsselwörter, die dir bei der Auswahl der richtigen Aussage helfen. Achte besonders auf Modalverben wie *must / must not, can/cannot, have to, …* usw.

Im ersten Beispiel könnten folgende Schlüsselwörter markiert werden: *crime – community – don't leave (things) – in car – report emergencies to police.* Hier geht es also um die Vermeidung von <u>Verbrechen</u> in der <u>Gemeinde</u>. Du sollst <u>(Dinge) nicht im Auto lassen</u> und im <u>Notfall die Polizei informieren</u>.

Mit dieser Vorgehensweise kannst du die falschen Aussagen sehr schnell erkennen.

Reading Part 2: British Music Festivals

TASKS

All the people below would like to go to a music festival.

- First read the information about them, then look at the different festivals on the next page.
- Find **two** possible festivals for each of the people below.
- Some festivals can be chosen more than once.
- Write the letters of the festivals in the boxes next to the right person.

No.	Festival 1	Festival 2		The people
6/7				a) **Cameron** lives in London and loves festivals but would like to get away from the mainstream big acts of rock. He loves electronic dance stuff and chill-out music and a bit of folk and jazz. He doesn't want to travel and can't afford more than £ 60 for a ticket, so for him a festival should be in the city.
8/9				b) **Rebecca** would like to have a weekend away from the big city, seeing some great rock bands and enjoying the atmosphere and the music with other people. She can spend up to £ 200 on this. Unfortunately she won't have time to attend a festival in August because she is starting a new job then.
10/11				c) **Ben** is a festivalgoer who loves all kinds of music – from metal to folk. Now that he is a bit older, music isn't everything. He doesn't want the big crowds and the fast food anymore. He'd prefer something different, with some theatre or the arts. He'd love to take his wife and his little two-year-old child for a festival weekend away in the countryside.
12/13				d) **Megan**, an American student, is spending a year in London and wants to experience a British music festival, but she hates camping in the countryside. She is into folk music and mainstream rock or pop. She likes making music, too. She'd like a festival day or weekend, preferably in London or in another city.
14/15				e) **Liam** loves big festivals with loud music, crowds of people, many different bands, big and famous names, camping in the field – the whole experience. He is prepared to pay quite a lot of money for that. He doesn't like all those arty family festivals with films, talks, etc. For him the perfect festival has to be two or three days of music and partying!

A	**Wilderness Festival; 12–14 August; adults – £ 99 / family ticket – £ 200** This is a very different kind of festival. Far away from the usual crowds and the camping in the dirt, it offers music, food, learning, literature and theatre – all set among the beautiful lakes and parkland of Oxfordshire. Great musicians, theatre artists and celebrated restaurant chefs create this unique experience. Activities for the whole family are organised, including nature walks and boating. Little ones can make use of the children's area with babysitting and games.
B	**Field Day; tickets on sale from £ 25.00** An Indie one-day festival with a dash of electro and dubstep. It is based in Victoria Park, East London, usually organised in early August. Dance acts will get you into the groove on three different stages. As well as all the amazing music, Field Day's off-the-wall Village Green area, 'Village Mentality', will supply plenty of good food and drink.
C	**Isle of Wight Festival; 11–12 June; weekend with camping – £ 165.00** Big and friendly festival that mixes famous mainstream rock bands like the Foo Fighters or U2 with newer independent artists and bands – so there's something for everyone. Friendly crowds, great atmosphere, good parties and fantastic countryside. What a weekend!
D	**Bloodstock Open Air; 11–15 August; full weekend with camping – £ 105** The best metal and heavy rock acts from across the globe, over 12,000 fans in a field – that is what you can expect at Bloodstock in August for a weekend of loud and unspoilt heavy metal! Over 100 artists including metal legends like Motörhead will perform on three stages over three days.
E	**The Bath Folk Festival; 8–14 August; workshop tickets from £ 75** The Bath Folk Festival is a seven-day event with live concerts by over 60 acts from all over the world. You can also take part in workshops or music summer schools in many different places all across the city of Bath. Listen to music or even learn to play folk music with some of the best musicians in the scene.
F	**Latitude Festival; 14–17 July; weekend camping – £ 177.00; day ticket £ 76.00** The best one when it comes to combining music, art, dance and poetry. A variety of musical artists, including some big names and bands, a friendly atmosphere with green fields for camping and lots of things to do for typical festivalgoers and families – from all-night parties to art talks and activities for the whole family or home-made food from the nearby farms. All this set in the beautiful green spaces of Henham Park, Southwold.
G	**Wireless Festival; 1–3 July; weekend £ 104.25, day tickets £ 54.25** A festival you can get to by bus – right in Hyde Park, the heart of London. So there's no muddy field and no need to sleep in a tent. Every year this festival offers amazing line-ups with the biggest names of rock and pop. This is the big one you shouldn't miss!
H	**Finnstock (Tickets available now at just £ 7.50 from Tamesis Dock)** Festivals these days are all too expensive, over-hyped and miles away. But this one is different. Finnstock is back in London in August. Right in the middle of the Thames. No big names of mainstream music, but all the best new London bands will be there. Finnstock has everything any festivalgoer needs.

LÖSUNGSHILFEN

Die Aufgabenstellung verrät dir bereits, dass du für jede der vorgestellten Personen zwei Festivals aus dem Angebot A bis H auswählen sollst, die seinen/ihren Interessen und Vorlieben entsprechen.

Dazu ist es unerlässlich, dass du im ersten Arbeitsschritt wichtige Informationen (= Schlüsselwörter) in der jeweiligen Personenbeschreibung markierst. Schlüsselwörter können hier z. B. das Alter, der Musikgeschmack, die Preisvorstellung oder der gewünschte Veranstaltungsort sein.

Bei Person 1 (Cameron) bieten sich beispielsweise folgende Begriffe an: *electronic, chill-out music, folk, jazz, no travel, (no more than) £ 60, in city (London)* – Auf diese Weise kannst du bereits gezielt nach preiswerten Festivals in London suchen. Die Auswahl beschränkt sich so schnell auf B,G und H. Der Musikgeschmack grenzt anschließend die Auswahl (B und H) weiter ein.

*Reading Part 3: The Flash Mob Phenomenon?

TASKS

- Read the text and the statements on the opposite page.
- Put a tick in the box next to the correct statement.
- For each task only one statement is correct.

The phenomenon of the flash mob – masses of people who meet suddenly and only for a short moment in a public place for an unusual or strange perfomance – began in 2003 and quickly spread to cities all across the world. Flash mobs are organised through the internet / social media like Facebook, Twitter or viral emails. There have been many examples of popular flash   5 mobs in recent years.

A well known one was the April 2006 Silent Disco in London. At various London underground stations, people gathered with their MP3 players and started dancing to their music at the same set time. It was reported that more than 4,000 people were dancing silently at London Victoria station alone.   10 Worldwide Pillow Fight Day followed in March 2008. Over 25 cities around the globe took part in the first "international flash mob", which was the world's largest flash mob to date. According to *The Wall Street Journal*, more than 5,000 people participated and threw pillows at one another in New York City. The event was organised via social network-   15 ing sites, private blogs as well as by word of mouth, text messaging and email. Participating cities included Atlanta, Budapest, Chicago, Copenhagen, Melbourne, New York, Paris, Shanghai, Zurich and many more.

Then there was 29 August 2009, when around 13,000 people met in Mexico City to celebrate Michael Jackson's 51st birthday by dancing to his song   20 "Thriller".

Although these spontaneous public meetings are usually organised as peaceful events, some of them are becoming troublesome. In a number of cities, flash mobs have led to vandalism.

Pizza shop owner Joey Rocco from Philadelphia has seen an out-of-control   25 flash mob first-hand. His pizza place is on South Street, in the heart of the city. It is a popular hangout for both kids and tourists. It was some weeks ago, and Rocco's pizza shop was filling up with customers. "We had the windows

open; it was a beautiful night," he says. "People were sitting in the window
30 areas, and I just happened to look out and said, 'Wow, the street is really
crowded.'" Some say the crowd of youths was in the hundreds. Others say
thousands. Rocco says the kids began to jump up and down, and then total
chaos broke out. Some of the teens started beating each other up, while others began banging on the windows of his shop. "They were trying to climb
35 into the windows and over the people who were dining, so we pushed them
out and we locked the front doors", he says. "Whatever they had in mind, to
me, it was like a home invasion."
In recent months Chicago police have also had many problems with what
they call "mob thefts". Large groups of teenagers repeatedly attacked stores on
40 Chicago's North Michigan Avenue – a busy shopping area. Usually between
five and as many as thirty 13- to 18-year-olds meet in front of a shop. They
flood inside, one of them gives a signal and then they all grab expensive goods,
designer wear or other things and disappear before the police arrive. Police
believe these shoplifting attacks are coordinated through text messages. Now
45 they have special officers monitoring social networking sites and others are
regularly patroling the shopping district. This strategy is beginning to show
results: the number of mob thefts in the area seems to be going down.
There are also cases of unintended flash mobs. It happened to a German teenage girl only recently. She put an invitation for her Sweet Sixteen Party on
50 Facebook and forgot to mark it as private. Despite public announcements that
the party was cancelled, over 1,500 guests made their way to her Hamburg
home, where local police tried to keep the crowd under control, while the
birthday girl had to hide somewhere else.

TASKS

16. Flash mobs …	A	started as a phenomenon in 2003.	☐
	B	were only popular for a short period of time.	☐
	C	are usually arranged with the help of the internet.	☐
	D	both A + C	☐

17. Silent Disco was an organised flash mob …	A	at a dance club that opened in 2006 underneath London Victoria underground station.	☐
	B	that saw people dancing to music which only they could hear on their MP3 players.	☐
	C	that happened at only one London tube station.	☐
	D	that saw 4,000 people dancing all over London.	☐

18. Worldwide Pillow Fight Day …	A	took place in America, Australia and Europe in 2008.	☐
	B	was the first known international flash mob.	☐
	C	was organised by Wall Street Journal.	☐
	D	both A + B	☐

19. On Worldwide Pillow Fight Day …	A	more people took part in a global flash mob than ever before.	☐
	B	thousands of people from over 25 cities came to New York to take part in a flash mob.	☐
	C	up to 5,000 people all over the world were throwing pillows at each other.	☐
	D	both B + C	☐

20. On 29 August 2009 …	A	Michael Jackson celebrated his 51st birthday in Mexico City.	☐
	B	13,000 people all over the world were dancing to "Thriller" at the same time.	☐
	C	many thousands of people were dancing to "Thriller" in Mexico City.	☐
	D	both A + B	☐

21. Joey Rocco's pizza place …	A	is outside the city center, in the south of Philadelphia.	☐
	B	doesn't normally attract a lot of tourists.	☐
	C	was quite busy on the evening of the incident.	☐
	D	doesn't allow customers to sit by the windows.	☐

22. Joey Rocco …	A	witnessed a flash mob that went violent.	☐
	B	organised a flashmob to make his pizza shop famous.	☐
	C	had over a thousand people in his pizza shop.	☐
	D	had to close his pizza shop down after a flash mob.	☐

23. Chicago …	A	has special shops for 13- to 18-year-olds on North Michigan Avenue.	☐
	B	has had problems with groups of teenagers who started robbing shops.	☐
	C	is the city where teenage groups attacked the local police department.	☐
	D	has a law that doesn't allow more than five teenagers at the same time into one shop.	☐

24. Chicago police ...	A	have policemen walking around in the shopping district.	☐
	B	have officers checking social media for signs of flash mob activities.	☐
	C	have managed to stop all mob thefts.	☐
	D	both A + B	☐

25. In Hamburg ...	A	a teenage girl planned her own flash mob birthday party.	☐
	B	over 1,500 guests turned up for a birthday party they had read about on Facebook.	☐
	C	some local policemen were invited to a party.	☐
	D	a birthday girl was very suprised when she opened her door to 1,500 guests.	☐

LÖSUNGSHILFEN

a) Vor dem Lesen:

Bereits die Überschrift verrät dir, dass es in diesem Text um Flashmobs geht, von denen du sicher schon gehört hast. Was weißt du bereits darüber? Worum könnte es gehen?

Mit dieser Erwartungshaltung solltest du alle Ankreuzmöglichkeiten gründlich durchlesen. Gibt es Lösungsvorschläge, die dir unwahrscheinlich erscheinen bzw. die du bereits im Vorfeld ausschließen kannst? Kennzeichne sie.

Markiere außerdem Schlüsselwörter der Lösungsvorgaben (z. B. „Silent Disco" oder „Chicago").

b) Beim Lesen:

Auch dieser Lesetext ist in verschiedene Abschnitte gegliedert. In der Regel widmet sich jeder Abschnitt einem Aspekt des Themas. Deine markierten Schlüsselwörter (z. B. „Silent Disco" oder „Chicago") finden sich in einzelnen (aufeinander folgenden) Abschnitten wieder. Lies also gezielt Abschnitt für Abschnitt.

Achtung: Bei einigen Aufgaben sind zwei Lösungsvorgaben richtig. Lies deshalb immer gründlich und versuche dich zu konzentrieren.

Writing Part 1: Your Photo

TASKS

You have posted this photo online. Your friend Paul wants to find out more about it.

- React to the comment and answer his questions.
- Write 40–50 words.

> Wow! Who's in the picture?
> Where was it taken?
> What's happening and
> how did it feel?

In the picture, you can see me, ~~it was~~ ~~my girlfriend where~~ My girlfriend take this photo and it feel so good. It feel when you do fly but swimming you inthe water.

/ 5 P.

LÖSUNGSHILFEN

Hier wirst du aufgefordert, anhand von Fragen einen zusammenhängenden Text bzw. Kommentar zu einem Foto zu formulieren. Vielleicht werden dir in der Prüfung mehrere Fotos zur Auswahl angeboten. Dann solltest du dich natürlich für das Bild entscheiden, zu dem dir inhaltlich und sprachlich am meisten einfällt. Du sollst dir vorstellen, du selbst hättest das Bild in einem sozialen Netzwerk gepostet. Du kannst also deine Fantasie nutzen und persönliche Ideen einbringen. Mache dir zu jeder Frage zunächst Notizen auf einem Extrablatt und formuliere sie anschließend aus.

TIPP (zu Writing Part 1)

Nutze bekannte Redemittel zur Bildbeschreibung (s. S. 97–98) und beachte die in den Fragen verwendeten Zeitformen und Wörter. Du kannst sie auch in deinen Antworten nutzen.

Writing Part 2: Getting Fit

TASKS

You have found this message posted on the internet.

- Write a letter to Sonny and answer his questions.
- Write between 100–160 words.
- Do not use internet slang.

Hey guys,
I really need your help. Summer is almost here and I'm not even happy about that.
I've spent the last three months sitting at home and studying for my final exams. I haven't been out in weeks. Now I'm feeling unfit, tired and a little out of shape. I have no energy and can't even run to catch the school bus.
My friends and family say I look as before, but I don't feel right. Maybe I should go on a diet? Or try some of these food supplement pills or powders? That might give me more energy ... I could also register with the local gym, but that's quite expensive.
What do you think is best? Have you ever felt like that? What do you do to keep fit? I'd love to hear your advice.
Thanks,
Sonny.

Hi Sonny,

_____

_____

_____

_____

_____

_____

_____

_____

_____

_____

_____

_____

_____

_____

_____

_____

_____

_____

_____

_____

Inhalt:	/ 6 P.	Sprache:	/ 6 P.	Gesamt:	/ 12 P.

INFO Punktverteilung Writing

Es kann sein, dass in deiner Prüfung die Punkte für *Writing* anders verteilt werden. Insgesamt wird es aber weiterhin 25 Punkte geben.

LÖSUNGSHILFEN

Diese Aufgabe erfordert einen längeren, zusammenhängenden Antworttext.
Die folgende Schrittfolge soll dir dein Vorgehen erleichtern:

1. Lies die Aufgabenstellung und markiere, **was** (einen Antworttext) du **wem** (Sonny) in **welchem Umfang** (100–160 Wörter) schreiben sollst.
2. Lies nun Sonnys Text durch. Unterstreiche seine Fragen an dich.
3. Fertige auf einem separaten Blatt eine Ideensammlung zu den fünf Fragen an. Wenn du mindestens ein bis zwei Ideen zur Beantwortung jeder Frage notiert hast, schreibe deine Antwort.
4. Achte auf den Textaufbau (siehe S. 17): Kennzeichne Einleitung, Hauptteil, Abschluss und Grußformel durch Absätze.
5. Lies dir nach der Fertigstellung des Textes abschließend deine Antwort noch einmal in Ruhe durch. Vielleicht findest du so noch den einen oder anderen Schreibfehler.

★ **Writing Part 3: Mediation – Options after School**

TASKS

You've received this message from an English-speaking friend:

Hi everybody. I'm in my last year at school and have no clue what to do after my exams.
I'd love to do something different and see more of the world. Any ideas welcome. Thanks, Phil.

• Read the two reports you have found online.
• Choose **one** report.
• Write an email to Phil and tell him about it.
• Say what the person you chose did and mention at least four aspects of their experience.
• Do not translate word for word.
• Write complete sentences.

Josephine, Freiwilligendienst in Peru

Mir war am Ende der zehnten Klasse schnell klar, dass ich nach der Schule nicht sofort an die Uni wollte. Ich wollte etwas ganz anderes erleben, eine andere Kultur, ein anderes Land. Zudem wollte ich meine Spanischkenntnisse gern nutzen und verbessern.

Im Internet fand ich ein dreimonatiges Projekt in Cusco, Peru. Nachdem ich Bilder sah und Berichte von anderen Freiwilligen gelesen hatte, war meine Entscheidung gefallen. Jetzt bin ich seit einem Monat hier und sammle täglich fantastische Erfahrungen. Meine Gastfamilie hat mich sehr freundlich aufgenommen. Ich habe ein kleines, gemütliches Zimmer nicht weit von meinem Projektarbeitsplatz.

Das ist ein Kindergarten. Dort arbeite ich von ca. 9–13 Uhr an vier Tagen in der Woche. Ich helfe der Erzieherin, die dort für 16–20 Kinder verantwortlich ist. Meine Aufgaben sind es, mit den Kindern zu spielen, ihnen etwas vorzulesen – auf Spanisch und manchmal sogar auf Englisch –, mit ihnen Bilder zu malen und zu basteln. Gerade bereiten wir ein Fest für Eltern und andere Familienmitglieder vor. Das ist sehr kreativ.

An meinen freien Tagen reise ich durchs Land und lerne Menschen und Kultur kennen: Ich war sogar schon am Titicacasee in 4.000 m Höhe. Unglaublich! Außerdem mache ich noch einen Spanischkurs und einen Kochkurs. Die peruanische Küche ist fantastisch und ich hoffe, ich kann meine Familie zu Hause damit begeistern. Heimweh ist für mich kein großes Problem. Die drei Monate gehen viel zu schnell vorbei und zum Glück gibt es ja das Internet.

Ich bin jeden Tag froh über meine Entscheidung für den Freiwilligendienst und werde jetzt schon traurig, wenn ich an mein Abflugdatum denke. Die Erfahrungen hier werden mich auf jeden Fall auf meinem weiteren Lebensweg begleiten.

Felipe, Au-pair aus Spanien

Ich bin 18 und vor drei Monaten aus Spanien nach Deutschland gekommen. Ich wohne bei meiner Gastfamilie in Tempelhof, in Berlin.

Irgendwie kam meine Entscheidung, Au-pair zu werden, ganz plötzlich. Ich war mit der Schule fertig und hatte noch keine Ausbildung.

Außerdem wollte ich mehr von der Welt sehen und hatte in der Schule Deutsch gelernt. Also dachte ich – warum nicht Deutschland? Meine Freunde waren überrascht – Au-pair – das ist doch Mädchensache ... Aber warum? Ich habe vier kleine Geschwister zu Hause – dann lernt man schon mit Kindern umzugehen.

Am Anfang war da schon ein bisschen Kulturschock – mein Deutsch war längst nicht so gut, wie ich dachte. Aber wir haben uns zu Hause irgendwie mit Händen und Füßen verständigt. Meine Gastmutter kann zum Glück auch etwas Spanisch. Natürlich habe ich gleich einen Deutschkurs begonnen und jeden Abend drei Stunden gelernt. Das hat geholfen. Mit meinen Gastkindern komme ich sehr gut klar – zwei Jungen im Alter von 5 und 8. Da ist vielleicht auch ein männlicher Au-pair ganz gut. Wir spielen zusammen, ich hole sie von der Kita oder Schule ab, wir machen Hausaufgaben und ich helfe im Haus beim Aufräumen und Einkaufen – eigentlich genauso wie in meiner Familie in Spanien. Außerdem habe ich Zeit, Berlin und Deutschland kennen zu lernen. An freien Abenden gehe ich gern ins Theater oder treffe mich mit meinen neuen deutschen Freunden. Letzte Woche waren wir in Dresden und haben die Stadt besichtigt, und in zwei Wochen nimmt mich meine Gastfamilie mit an die Ostsee. Nur jetzt im Herbst vermisse ich das Wetter in Spanien.

Ich würde die Au-pair-Tätigkeit definitiv empfehlen – auch für Jungen. Man lernt viel über andere Kulturen und sich selbst, wird unabhängiger, ist aber trotzdem Teil einer Familie.

_____
_____
_____
_____
_____
_____
_____
_____
_____
_____
_____
_____
_____
_____
_____
_____
_____
_____
_____
_____
_____
_____
_____
_____
_____
_____
_____
_____
_____

Inhalt:	/ 4 P.	Sprache:	/ 4 P.	Gesamt:	/ 8 P.

LÖSUNGSHILFEN

Bei der Lösung dieser Mediationsaufgabe helfen dir die folgenden Schritte:

1. Lies die Aufgabenstellung genau durch und markiere dir:
   Zu welchem Zweck **(warum?)** sollst du Informationen in die englische Sprache übertragen? (Hier ist es das Ziel, eine E-Mail zu verfassen, in der du dem Schüler Phil ein Auslandsprojekt beschreibst, an dem er nach Beendigung der Schule teilnehmen kann.)
   Was soll beschrieben werden? (Du sollst beschreiben, was die von dir ausgewählte Person im Ausland tat sowie mindestens vier Aspekte bzw. Erfahrungen benennen, die für die Person damit verbunden waren.)

2. Du sollst also aus zwei Berichten einen auswählen, von dem du Phil erzählst.
   Lies nun mit dieser Fragestellung beide Texte in Ruhe durch.

3. Deine Auswahl sollte die sprachlichen Anforderungen der beiden Texte berücksichtigen.
   Prüfe, welchen Text du recht gut ins Englische übertragen könntest.
   Wo schätzt du deine Kenntnisse in Bezug auf die erforderlichen sprachlichen Mittel besser ein?
   Gibt es einen Text, bei dem du auf den ersten Blick erkennst, dass du viele der wichtigen Hauptwörter (Nomen, Verben, Adjektive) nicht übersetzen könntest? Dann entscheide dich gegen ihn.

4. Markiere nun in dem ausgewählten Text **wichtige** Informationen.
   Die fünf W-Fragen können dir dabei helfen: **Wer**, **Wo**, **Wann**, **Was**, **Wie**?

5. Nimm einen Schmierzettel und übertrage diese Informationen, die du zu den W-Fragen ermittelt hast, ins Englische. Nutze die Arbeitstechniken auf Seite 18, um unbekannte Wörter zu umschreiben. Denk daran, dass du nicht jede Information wortwörtlich übersetzen musst!

6. Schreibe nun deinen Antwortbrief. Schreibe **vollständige** englische Sätze.

A3 Angeleiteter Test 2

Teil I: Hörverstehen

Listening Part 1: Voicemail Messages

 Track 5

TASKS

You are going to hear three voicemail messages.
There is one question each for the first two messages and two questions for the third message.

- Look at the pictures and listen to the recording.
- Choose the correct picture and put a tick in the right box.
- You can listen to the recording twice.

Voicemail Message 1

1. Which picture is the speaker reacting to?

A ☐

B ☒ ✓

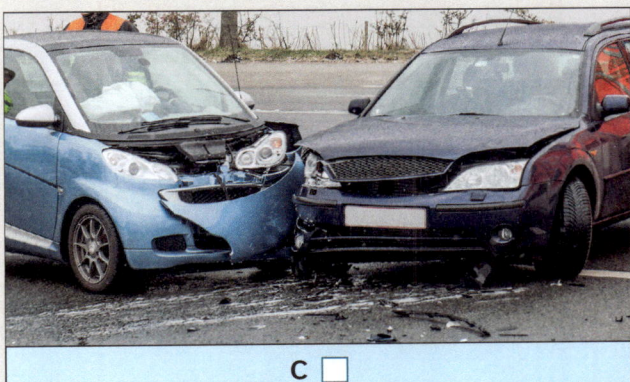

C ☐

D ☐

_____

_____

_____

_____

Voicemail Message 2

3. Which picture is the speaker reacting to?

A ☒

B ☐

C ☐

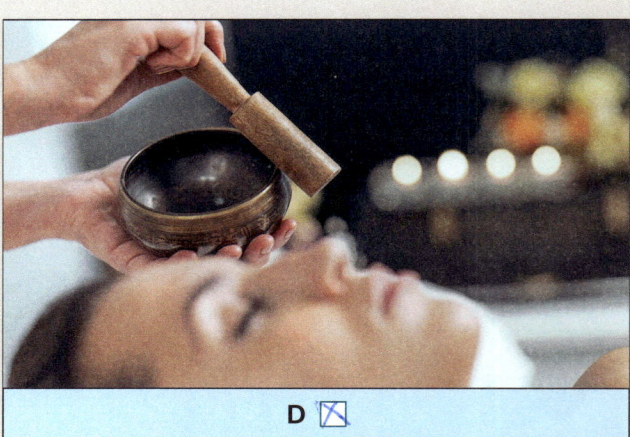

D ☒ ✓

_____

_____

_____

_____

Voicemail Message 3

3. Which picture is the speaker sending?

A ☐

B ☐

C ☒ ✓

D ☒

_____
_____
_____
_____

4. What time are they meeting?

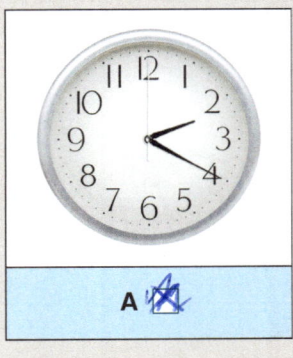

A ☒

B ☒

C ☒

D ☐

_____
_____
_____
_____

LÖSUNGSHILFEN

314

In dieser Aufgabe geht es darum, Sprachnachrichten im Detail zu verstehen. Die folgende Schrittfolge wird dir helfen, diese Aufgabe zum Hörverstehen erfolgreich zu lösen:

1. Lies die Aufgabenstellung und die Fragen zunächst in Ruhe durch. Schau dir die Bilder gut an.
2. Beschrifte die Bilder auf den Schreiblinien mit Schlüsselwörtern, auf die du im Hörtext achten solltest. Schreib z. B. die Uhrzeiten an die Uhren und sprich sie dir leise vor. So fällt es dir leichter, alles zu verstehen.
3. Generell gilt: Keine Panik, wenn du beim ersten Hören nicht jedes Detail verstehst!
   Beim zweiten Durchgang wirst du die fehlenden Informationen ganz sicher ergänzen können.

instead of = anstand

Listening Part 2: Radio Spots

 **Track 6**

TASKS

You are going to hear four radio spots.

- Read the six slogans below first.
- Choose the right slogan for each spot from the list and put a tick under the right letter (A–F) in the grid.
- There is only one slogan for each spot. Two slogans cannot be matched.
- You will hear the recording twice.

A) Adopt a runaway kid and help them to a new life.

B) Adopt your favourite animal and support your local zoo.

C) Don't let social media spoil your life.

D) Show up and enjoy your local art and music scene.

E) Use your local market and support your community.

F) Watch out for the missing and help to unite families again.

Number	Radio Spot	A	B	C	D	E	F	
5	Radio Spot 1						✗	✓
6	Radio Spot 2			✗				✓
7	Radio Spot 3	✗	✗					✓
8*	Radio Spot 4				✗			✓

LÖSUNGSHILFEN

Hier sollen die Hauptaussagen von vier Radiospots verstanden werden. Die folgenden Tipps helfen dir, dich auf Wesentliches zu konzentrieren:

Lies die Aufgabenstellung und die Slogans genau durch. Markiere Schlüsselwörter (Nomen und Verben), die dir später beim Hören als Signalwörter dienen und die dir das Textverständnis erleichtern können. Achte beim Hören auch darauf, an wen sich der Spot richtet, d. h., wer tatsächlich angesprochen wird.

Listening Part 3: A Great Barrier Reef Day Cruise

 **Track 7**

TASKS

- You are going to hear part of a guided tour of the Great Barrier Reef.
- Complete the table below using keywords and phrases.
- You can listen to the recording twice.

facts about the size of the reef (2):	one activity on the tour:
9. _3000 seperate_	14. _seeing many aniwills_
10. _2000 km long_	

sea life around the reef (2 examples):	what you learn about corals:
11. _dolpinc & fish_	15. _7 biggest in the World_
12. _____	

number of visitors every year:	rule for divers at the reef:
13. _____	16. _____

LÖSUNGSHILFEN

Bei dieser Aufgabe solltest du dir vor dem Hören unbedingt die Überschrift und die in der Tabelle vorgegebenen Aspekte durchlesen, um zu erfassen, worauf du genau achten sollst. Es geht um das Great Barrier Reef in Australien. Weißt du bereits etwas darüber? Welche Meeresbewohner wird es dort vermutlich geben? Was, glaubst du, dürfen Taucher dort nicht tun? Überlege, welche englischen Wörter und Begriffe du in diesem Zusammenhang erwartest.

Beim ersten Hören bewahre Ruhe. Du musst auch hier nicht alles sofort verstehen. Markiere nach dem ersten Hören die Kästchen, auf die du beim zweiten Durchgang noch einmal genauer achten musst. Es kann sein, dass du mehrere Antwortmöglichkeiten heraushörst und gar nicht alle benötigst. Dann entscheide dich für die Antwort, die dir am sichersten erscheint.

*Listening Part 4: Teenage Ganglands

 Track 8

TASKS

You are going to hear part of a radio talk about teenage gangs.
There are four people talking: a presenter, Edna, Matt and Pauline.

- Read the statements below and listen to the recording.
- Put a tick in the box next to the correct statement.
- In each task only one statement is correct.
- You can listen to the recording twice.

17. One of the studio guests on the show ...	A	is a thirteen-year-old teenager from Hackney.	☐
	B	works in a prison for criminal teenagers.	☐
	C	has written a book about teenage gangs.	☒ ✓

18. There are reports of ...	A	over 150 violent knife attacks in different London areas last year.	☐
	B	growing problems with teenage knife attacks and active youth gangs.	☒ ✓
	C	over 150 gangs operating in different London areas.	☒ ✓

19. Pauline joined the gang ...	A	because her mother had left the family.	☐
	B	when she was 13 years old.	☒ ✓
	C	because her boyfriend got her into it.	☐

20. Edna worries about her son Jamie ...	A	because he goes out and doesn't tell her what he's doing.	☐ ✓
	B	because she lost her older son in a gang fight when he was 13.	☒
	C	because he has been in many fights at school.	☐

21. Matt thinks that ...	A	Jamie's behaviour is quite normal and not that worrying.	☐
	B	teenagers who don't talk much to their parents are at risk of becoming a gang member.	☒
	C	it's normal for teenagers to change their style and all their friends quite often and quite suddenly.	☐

22. Edna says that …	A	she and Jamie often argue or fight at home.	☐
	B	Jamie suddenly had a lot of money.	☒
	C	she hasn't seen Jamie with a new phone or other gadget recently.	☐

23. Pauline's gang …	A	made her feel like she was part of a big family.	☐
	B	stole a few little things but never acted violently.	☐
	C	specialised in stealing mobile phones.	☒

24. Pauline thinks that Edna …	A	should buy Jamie a new mobile phone so that she can always contact him.	☐
	B	should check on Jamie more often and watch all his actions closely.	☐
	C	shouldn't worry too much about her son and should give him some freedom.	☒ ✓

25. Pauline …	A	was lucky that she was still at school and didn't have to go to prison.	☒
	B	has been in prison and is now working with young people and children.	☑ ✓
	C	is still a gang member but is trying to get out with community help.	☐

LÖSUNGSHILFEN

Die Überschrift und die Aufgabenstellung verraten dir bereits, dass es im folgenden Hörtext um eine Radiodiskussion zum Thema „Jugendbanden/Jugendgangs" gehen wird. Stelle dich gedanklich auf dieses Thema ein und lies nun die Lösungsvorgaben genau durch. Nur eine der Aussagen stimmt jeweils.
Auch hier hilft es, Schlüsselwörter (Nomen, Verben, Ziffern/Zahlen) farbig hervorzuheben. Im ersten Beispiel wird es dir so leichter fallen herauszuhören, ob der Sprecher über 150 Messerattacken oder doch eher über 150 Jugendgangs berichtet. Versuche dich beim ersten Hören an die unterschiedlichen Stimmen der Sprechenden zu gewöhnen, damit es dir leichter fällt, sie zu erkennen und ihnen die Aussagen zuzuordnen.

4 / 3

Teil II: Leseverstehen/Schreiben

Reading Part 1: Travelling Around – Signs and Notices

TASKS

- Read the text of each sign.
- Read the four statements next to it and decide which statement matches the sign.
- Tick the right statement. Only one of them is correct.

1. London Underground Safety Notice

Please stand on the right of the escalators, hold the handrail and keep clear of the edges. Take care of children. Dogs must be carried.

A	This sign warns you about dangerous dogs.	☐
B	This sign tells you how to use the escalator safely.	☐
C	This sign warns you that children shouldn't use the escalator.	☐
D	You can't take dogs on the escalator.	☐

2. London Underground

 Bicycles are not permitted on the London Underground between 07.30 and 09.30 and between 16.00 and 19.00 on weekdays and cannot be taken on the moving escalators.

At all other times you can take bicycles on the designated sections of the trains.

A	This sign tells you where to park your bike.	☐
B	Bikes are generally not allowed on the London underground.	☐
C	The escalators don't work weekday mornings and afternoons.	☐
D	On Sundays you can take your bike on an underground train all day.	☐

3. At a Greater London train station

Have you paid? If you cannot produce a valid ticket when asked by a ticket inspector, you will be charged a penalty fare of £ 20 or double the amount of a single ticket. So do not forget to buy a ticket before you travel.

A	You should buy a ticket before you get on the train.	☐
B	You can buy your ticket on the train.	☐
C	You can only buy single tickets over £ 20 on the train.	☐
D	There are no ticket inspectors on the trains.	☐

4. At the airport

Can your hand luggage travel with you? Then it should
• be light enough for you to carry and lift without help.
• not contain any sharp, dangerous or explosive items, e. g. knives, gas lighters, scissors etc.
• not contain any liquids over the permitted 100 ml amount.

A	You shouldn't lift heavy hand luggage without help.	☐
B	You can't carry knives or scissors in your hand luggage.	☐
C	Your hand luggage shouldn't weigh more than 500g.	☐
D	You can carry as much liquid as you like with you, but only in your hand luggage.	☐

5. In a hotel room

We will provide you
with fresh towels every day. But remember, washing and drying towels uses a lot of energy. So help to save energy by using your towels again. If you want your towels replaced, leave the used ones on the floor.

A	If you reuse your towels, you can help the environment.	☐
B	You can't have fresh towels every day.	☐
C	These towels are not good for drying.	☐
D	You can use these towels for drying the floor.	☐

LÖSUNGSHILFEN

Diese Art der Zuordnungsaufgabe ist dir bereits bekannt. Du weißt, dass es hier darauf ankommt, die korrekte Aussage des Hinweisschildes aus einem Angebot von vier Vorgaben auszuwählen.

Der Teufel steckt hier wieder im Detail. Achte deshalb auf die folgende Schrittfolge:

1. Lies das Schild genau durch.

2. Markiere in den Lösungsvorgaben Schlüsselwörter

   Bsp. 1)

   A: *warn – dangerous dogs*

   B: *how – use escalator*

   C: *children – not – use escalator*

   D: *not take – dogs – on escalator*

3. Finde und markiere ähnliche Formulierungen im Schild / der Bekanntmachung und den Aussagen daneben:

   Bsp. 5): *save energy by using towels again = reuse your towels, help the environment*

Bei dieser Vorgehensweise erkennst du sehr schnell, welche Aussage jeweils die richtige ist.

Reading Part 2: The Perfect Job

All the people below would like to work.

- First read the information about them, then look at the different jobs on the next page.
- Find **two** possible jobs for each of the people below.
- You can choose some jobs more than once.
- Write the letters of the jobs in the boxes next to the right person.

No.	Job 1	Job 2		The people
6/7				**Lauren** has just had a child. She wants to start working again but would prefer evening work so she can look after her child during the day. Lauren would be happy with part-time work. She used to be a bus driver, so a driving job would be great. She has good social skills and is also happy working with people.
8/9				**Martin** wants to find paid work for which he doesn't have to sit in one place all day. He doesn't mind irregular working hours, but it shouldn't be a tiring outdoor job. Martin has a driving licence and speaks French fluently. He enjoys contact with people but doesn't want to work with teenagers or kids.
10/11				**Kylie** is training to be a teacher and would like to get some more experience before she starts the final year of her course. She loves working with children and young people and is quite flexible with her working times. Pay is less important to her than finding the right kind of work.
12/13				**Kevin** doesn't mind what job he does as long as it is full-time and pays well. He is planning to go to Australia after the summer, so he needs money for this. He also wants to earn enough money to do his driving licence. He has no problem getting his hands dirty doing physical work.
14/15				**Alice** is a French student living in London. She'd like to work at weekends or during her summer holidays. Pay is important because London is expensive. Alice wants to work with other people. She is prepared to do all kinds of things – teaching, office work or hard, physical work. However, she doesn't drive and she doesn't feel confident with teenagers and young adults.

A) Farm help needed
Who wants to spend a summer month on a Kent farm and earn good money? If you are not afraid of hard work – from feeding animals to working the fields – come and work for us! We offer good pay, food and farm accommodation. We are also known for our lively and friendly working atmosphere, as we always have ten or more farm helpers from different places.

B) Summer Camp
Summer camp for young people (aged 12 to 16) with difficult social backgrounds is looking for volunteers. Make a difference – work with young people, organise activities like boating or games and have fun. This could be a unique experience for anybody who loves working with people and a great addition to your CV. The pay is basic, but we also offer free food and accommodation in the camp.

C) Help!
My husband and I have just found out that we have to move to France in September. So we need help – help with packing all our stuff here and help with getting organised in France. Can you teach us a bit of French? Can you help us understand and write letters in French? And are you organised enough to help us with the packing? If you could spare one or two days a week or a weekend instead, that'd be great. Some help with driving to France is also needed. Good pay is guaranteed.

D) Food delivery
We are looking for flexible, reliable people to deliver sandwiches to our late-night stores in the evenings and at some weekends. A valid driving licence is necessary. No heavy lifting is involved. Good pay.

E) Restaurant Manager
Evening help needed. "The Alternative Restaurant" is a project run by teenagers and young adults who have been in trouble with the police. We are looking for someone with good people skills who can help organise these young workers in the restaurant. No cooking skills needed. Three to four evenings a week. Fair pay.

F) Looking for hard-working cleaners
Cleaning company looking for help in a large office building during the summer. This is hard, physical work. You will often work on your own, so you must be a self-motivator. Good pay and lots of extra hours of work available for the right person.

G) Office help needed
A travel company which specialises in holidays to France is looking for someone to help us in our office. The successful applicant will have good French and English skills. We are a friendly team and offer good pay. This is a summer job only.

LÖSUNGSHILFEN

In dieser Zuordnungsaufgabe geht es darum, für fünf Menschen jeweils zwei passende Jobs auszuwählen. Um diese Aufgabe zügig und erfolgreich zu lösen, solltest du dir zunächst die Beschreibungen der einzelnen Personen (S. 48) durchlesen und Schlüsselwörter farbig markieren. Als Schlüsselwörter gelten hier Informationen, die für die Wahl eines Jobs wesentlich sind, z. B. gewünschte Arbeitszeiten, Interessen und Gehaltsvorstellungen. Bei Lauren, der ersten Person, könnten das folgende Informationen sein: „evening work", „part-time", „driving", „good social skills", „with people". Nun suche entsprechende Informationen in den Jobangeboten. Wo findest du die meisten Übereinstimmungen? Denke daran, dass vielleicht auch nicht alle Fähigkeiten der Jobsuchenden zum Einsatz kommen müssen. Wichtig ist, dass du eventuelle Ausschlusskriterien überprüfst.

*Reading Part 3: Students Demand Green New Deal for Schools

Students at more than 50 high schools in the USA have joined together in a campaign to demand that their local education authorities do more to educate young people in high schools about climate change.

Darja Corsin, a high school student from Jacksonville, Oregon explained what
5 has motivated her to be part of this protest movement: "Local education authorities and school boards are simply not doing enough to inform students about the climate crisis. Indeed, in some districts, the authorities have removed books that explain global warming from school libraries."

The campaign has bundled a series of demands into what it calls a "Green New
10 Deal for Schools". Most importantly, the campaigners are calling for better education about climate change. But it doesn't stop there. They also demand that high schools offer careers advice about how to get into green jobs after graduation and that they draw up action plans for dealing with climate disasters, for example flooding, hurricanes and heatwaves. Indeed, the campaign
15 goes even further and demands that school buildings should be overhauled to make them more climate-resilient and that school lunches should be made from locally sourced ingredients.

As forest fires and storms caused severe problems over the summer in NW and central USA, Texas and Georgia, students returned to high school deter-
20 mined to engage in depth with the topic of climate change and the destructive impact of fossil fuels.

However, they face the problem that in some US states, local laws discourage schools from dealing with "divisive" topics. This means that topics on which there are very different points of view are excluded from the curriculum or
25 only dealt with if both sides of the argument are clearly presented. When it comes to climate change, this means that in some states the advantages of fossil fuels have to be explained just as much as the dangers of global warming. Topics such as climate justice are often suppressed entirely.

Students in Georgia, Texas, Florida and Idaho, for example, argue that this is
30 a problem in their states. They take the view that there is a global consensus that fossil fuels are not the future and that we have to move onto renewable energy as quickly as we can. So, in their opinion, it makes no sense to spend time in class discussing the advantages of oil and gas. Esther Lavron, a 16-year-old student at South Stowe High School in Blue Ridge, Georgia, sums up the
35 problem as follows: "At school, most teachers have avoided discussions about any topics that could be considered political, including climate justice. Basically, we don't learn about climate change at all."

Jesper Matthews, a 15-year-old student at a high school in Deptford, Philadelphia, points out some of the practical disadvantages of inaction by local
40 authorities. When he returned to high school after the summer break, there

was still a severe heatwave in Philadelphia. The campus buildings have no air conditioning, so the students were sent home early and all sports practice and games were cancelled. "It's scary to be faced with this", he says. "Basically, our campus isn't a safe and healthy place to be."

The campaign is already having an effect. Later this week, a large number of students will meet with Ed Markey, the senator for Massachusetts, in Washington DC to mark the introduction of a proposed new law. The law, if it is passed by Congress and the US Senate, will be called the Green New Deal for Public Schools Act. Over the next decade this legislation would provide funding of over $ 1.4 trillion to help schools improve education and face the climate crisis. The money would be used to expand the curriculum to include climate change, to hire new teachers and to adapt campus buildings to cope with the effects of adverse weather conditions. It would also help create many jobs, especially in poorer and more vulnerable communities, taking on environmental and racial inequities, making schools safer, healthier and environmentally friendlier places.

TASKS

16. What has motivated Darja Corsin to be part of the protest movement?	A	A lack of extracurricular activities in high schools.	☐
	B	A lack of information about the climate crisis in high schools.	☐
	C	Inadequate cafeteria food in high schools.	☐
	D	Books in school libraries that don't explain global warming well.	☐

17. What is the main focus of the "Green New Deal for Schools"?	A	Demanding better education about climate change in high schools.	☐
	B	Offering free textbooks for high school students.	☐
	C	Providing scholarships for students who plan to go on to college.	☐
	D	both A + C	☐

18. What else are the activists campaigning for?	A	Providing school lunches made from locally grown products.	☐
	B	Drawing up an action plan for dealing with climate extremes.	☐
	C	Offering courses on food and food preparation.	☐
	D	both A + C	☐

19. Why do students in some states like Georgia, Texas, Florida and Idaho consider the handling of climate change in their schools problematic?	A	Schools lack funding for extracurricular activities.	☐
	B	There is not enough democracy or student involvement in school decisions.	☐
	C	Local laws make it difficult for schools to discuss issues such as climate change.	☐
	D	The infrastructure in schools is inadequate and they don't have qualified teachers.	☐

20. What viewpoint is shared by students in Georgia, Texas, Florida, and Idaho regarding the discussion of fossil fuels in school?	A	Fossil fuels are the future and should be encouraged.	☐
	B	Fossil fuels have both advantages and disadvantages, but there's no alternative.	☐
	C	The dangers of global warming are mostly exaggerated.	☐
	D	There is worldwide agreement that fossil fuels mustn't be used in the future.	☐

21. What does Esther Lavron say is the problem at her school?	A	The teachers don't believe in climate change.	☐
	B	The students don't learn anything in classes.	☐
	C	The students aren't politically aware or interested.	☐
	D	Teachers are unwilling to deal with topics like climate change.	☐

22. Why did students in Philadelphia have to leave school early and cancel sports activities?	A	There was a lack of interest in sports among students.	☐
	B	There was some extreme weather and it got too hot in the school buildings.	☐
	C	Many teachers got ill due to the heatwave, so they couldn't supervise sports activities.	☐
	D	There was a transport strike because of the heatwave.	☐

23. What impact is the campaign expected to have according to the text?	A	It will introduce a law to expand student numbers in high schools.	☐
	B	It will provide funding to decrease the number of teachers.	☐
	C	It will introduce a law called the Green New Deal for Public Schools Act.	☐
	D	It will close campus buildings that are not adapted to cope with weather extremes.	☐

24. If the Green New Deal for Public Schools Act becomes law, how much funding will it provide?	A	Almost $1.4 trillion.	☐
	B	At least $1.4 trillion, spread out over 10 years.	☐
	C	At least $1.4 trillion every year.	☐
	D	Exactly $1.4 trillion.	☐

25. Which of the uses of this public money mentioned in the final paragraph have not been mentioned earlier in the article?	A	Helping poor communities deal with racial inequality.	☐
	B	Making school buildings more climate-resilient.	☐
	C	Putting the topic of climate change in the school curriculum.	☐
	D	Making school buildings healthier places.	☐

LÖSUNGSHILFEN

Um die erforderlichen Textdetails zügig zu erfassen und die anschließenden Multiple-Choice-Aufgaben erfolgreich zu lösen, kann dir die folgende Schrittfolge behilflich sein:

1. Lies die **Überschrift** genau durch. Sie verrät dir bereits, worum es in diesem Text geht, nämlich um „High School Students" und einen „Green New Deal". Überlege dir im Voraus, was Teil dieses Themas sein könnte, z. B. Nachhaltigkeit an amerikanischen High Schools, das Thema Umwelt im Stundenplan und ähnliche Themen.

2. Mit diesem **Vorwissen** mache dich mit den Lösungsvorgaben vertraut. Gibt es Antwortmöglichkeiten, die dir absurd erscheinen oder die du auf Grund deines Vorwissens bereits ausschließen kannst? Markiere sie.

3. Suche und markiere **Schlüsselwörter/-wendungen**, wie z. B. *fossil fuels* oder *climate change* in den Antwortmöglichkeiten und auch im Text. Deine markierten Schlüsselwörter können in mehreren Textabschnitten vorkommen. Lies diese mehrfach bzw. besonders genau.

4. Bedenke, dass die Aufgabenabfolge in der Regel der Reihenfolge des Textes entspricht.

5. Sei besonders aufmerksam, wenn dir in der Aufgabenstellung mehrere richtige Antwortoptionen vorgeschlagen werden (z. B. „both A + B"). Lies hier alle Antwortmöglichkeiten noch einmal und gleiche sie mit der Textpassage ab, bevor du dich entscheidest. Falls wirklich zwei Antwortmöglichkeiten korrekt sind, bekommst du den Punkt nämlich nur, wenn du diese Option auswählst, selbst wenn du dich für eine der beiden richtigen Antworten entscheidest.

Writing Part 1: Your Photo

TASKS

You have posted this photo online. Your friend Cath wants to find out more about it.

- React to the comment and answer her questions.
- Write 40–50 words.

Wow!
Did you really do this?
Where was it taken?
Were you alone?
Did you enjoy it?

/ 5 P.

LÖSUNGSHILFEN

Auch bei diesem Foto ist es wichtig, sich zuerst einmal die dargestellte Situation genau anzuschauen. Was ist hier passiert, wer war dabei? Lass deiner Fantasie freien Lauf.

Notiere wieder alle Fragen auf einem Extrablatt und schreibe dir Ideen dazu auf. Diese Notizen kannst du nutzen, um deinen zusammenhängenden Text zu verfassen.

Writing Part 2: A Class Trip to Berlin

TASKS

You have found this message posted on the internet.

- Write a message to Gavin and answer his questions.
- Write between 100–160 words.
- Do not use internet slang.

Hi guys,
I'm in my final year at school and we're planning a last class trip.
My idea is Berlin. I've heard it's such a cool city.
So I need some insider tips:
– What would be a good time to visit Berlin?
– I'm sure it's a big city and we want to stay somewhere cool and
  central. So what's the best area for us to stay?
– Are there any dangerous places we should not go to?
– And what are the top three "must-sees" for teenagers like us in
  your opinion?
Please help, I'm waiting for your ideas.
Thanks, Gavin (16, from Dundee, Scotland)

Hi Gavin,

_____

_____

_____

_____

_____

_____

_____

_____

_____

_____

_____

_____

_____

_____

_____

_____

_____

_____

_____

_____
_____
_____
_____
_____
_____
_____
_____
_____
_____

Inhalt:	/ 6 P.	Sprache:	/ 6 P.	Gesamt:	/ 12 P.

LÖSUNGSHILFEN

Finde zunächst heraus, **wem** du **was** in **welcher Form** schreiben sollst. Markiere anschließend die Fragen in dem Post, auf die du in deinem Antwortschreiben eingehen sollst. Im nächsten Schritt notiere auf einem Extra-Blatt zu jeder Frage einige Ideen, die dir später das zügige Schreiben erleichtern.

Achte während des Schreibens darauf, dass du deinen Antworttext sinnvoll gliederst und die einzelnen Fragen in Abschnitten beantwortest. Vergiss nicht, deine Nachricht angemessen zu beenden (s. S. 17).

★ **Writing Part 3: Mediation – Summer Jobs**

TASKS

Your English-speaking friend Jazz would like to spend the summer holidays in Germany.
They love animals and are looking for a summer job. They have asked you for help.

- Read the two reports which you have found on the internet.
- Choose **one** report.
- Write an e-mail to your friend Jazz telling them about the kind of work they could do.
- Say what the farm assistant does and mention at least four aspects about the job with kids and/or animals.
- Do not translate word for word.
- Write complete sentences.

Jobben auf dem Reiterhof

Der Ferien- und Reiterhof Bendfeldt in Grömitz ist ein Familienbetrieb. Seit vielen Jahren werden auf dem Bauernhof Feriengäste betreut, die sich an der frischen Land- und Seeluft erholen wollen. Neben dem Hotelbetrieb betreibt die Familie aktive Landwirtschaft, Viehzucht und einen Reitbetrieb. Da fällt natürlich jede Menge Arbeit an, für die man Unterstützung sucht. Deshalb geben die Besitzer seit Jahren immer wieder jungen Helfern die Möglichkeit, die Arbeit auf dem Hof näher kennen zu lernen und tolle Erfahrungen für das Berufsleben zu sammeln. Im Vordergrund steht dabei der Pferdejob im Reitbetrieb. Die elf Ponys und Pferde müssen täglich versorgt werden und für das anstehende Kinderprogramm, den Reitunterricht oder Ausritte vorbereitet werden. Aber auch weitere spannende Aufgaben, die im täglichen Umgang mit den Pferden anfallen, warten dort auf dich. Als zusätzliches Extra kannst du nebenbei tolle Erfahrungen im pädagogischen Bereich sammeln, wenn du bei der Kinderbetreuung am Vor- und Nachmittag mithilfst.

Wie sieht dein Tag aus? Der Tag beginnt mit der Versorgung der Pferde am Morgen: das Füttern der Pferde, das Einstreuen der Ställe sowie die Vorbereitung der Ponys für die allmorgendlich stattfindende Ponyführrunde mit den Ferienkindern. Wenn du sehr gute Reiterfahrung hast, kannst du auch selbst bei Reitstunden helfen. Auch das Putzen und Waschen der Pferde, sowie das Raus- und Reinholen von der Wiese wird zu deinen täglichen Aufgaben gehören.

Natürlich kannst du auch Ausritte begleiten und bei guten Reitkenntnissen selbst reiten.

Quelle: https://www.farmarbeit.de/pferdejob-groemitz.html (aus didaktischen Gründen verändert)

Kinderbauernhof Haselsthal

Auf unserem Kinderbauernhof in Heinersdorf bei Berlin sind viele verschiedene Tiere zu Hause: Schafe, Ziegen, Ponys, Meerschweinchen und viele mehr, die unter deiner Anleitung von unseren kleinen Gästen versorgt werden. Die Kinder nehmen am Alltag auf dem Bauernhof teil und kümmern sich sowohl um das Füttern als auch das Pflegen der Tiere. Selbstverständlich wirst du vorab ausführlich in deine Aufgaben eingewiesen und hast jederzeit jemanden vor Ort, der dich unterstützt und dir Fragen beantwortet. Das Team sorgt aber nicht nur für das Wohlbefinden der Tiere, sondern auch für ein Wochenprogramm, das den Kindern viel Freude bereitet. Da kann auch hin und wieder ein wenig Kreativität nötig sein, wenn es mal regnet. Insgesamt können sich bis zu 35 Kinder zwischen 4 und 14 Jahren auf dem Hof tummeln. Ihre Nächte verbringen sie – wie auch die Betreuerinnen und Betreuer – in ihrem eigenen Schlafsack in einem unserer beiden Heuschober, der Villa Wolkenschiff oder der Ballenburg.

Wir freuen uns, wenn du uns unterstützen möchtest und du ...

– mindestens 18 Jahre alt bist;
– souverän, offen, belastbar und ein guter Teamplayer bist;
– dich in neuen Situationen schnell zurechtfindest;
– kein Problem damit hast, Verantwortung für dich und deine Schützlinge zu übernehmen;
– unseren kleinen Gästen auch mal helfen kannst, einen Streit zu lösen;
– dich für Tiere interessierst und es dir zutraust, den Kindern zu zeigen, wie man gewissenhaft mit ihnen umgeht und sie versorgt.

Eine kleine Vorwarnung vorab: mit Urlaub hat die Arbeit auf unserem Bauernhof wenig zu tun. Dennoch kannst du dir sicher sein, dass die Kinder und die Tiere dir ganz viel Zuneigung und Freude schenken werden. Darüber hinaus sind für dich Essen und Unterkunft natürlich kostenlos. Außerdem bekommst du 250 € für deine Reisekosten sowie weitere Ausgaben. Wir freuen uns auf dich!

_____

_____

_____

_____

_____

_____

_____

_____

_____

_____

_____

_____

_____

_____

_____

_____

_____

_____

_____

_____

_____

_____

_____

Inhalt:	/ 4 P.	Sprache:	/ 4 P.	Gesamt:	/ 8 P.

LÖSUNGSHILFEN

Finde zunächst heraus, zu welchem Zweck du welche Informationen ins Englische übertragen sollst. Auch hier geht es wieder darum, einen Text auszuwählen, in diesem Fall um einen Sommerjob für Jugendliche. Deine Aufgabe ist es, den Sommerjob deiner Wahl kurz zu benennen und durch vier wichtige Detailinformationen näher zu beschreiben.

Markiere nun die Hauptinformationen, bevor du sie auf einem Notizzettel ins Englische überträgst.

Die Tippsammlung (S. 18) verdeutlicht dir noch einmal Möglichkeiten, unbekannten Wortschatz in der Fremdsprache zu umschreiben.

A4 Test 3

Teil I: Hörverstehen

Listening Part 1: Voicemail Messages

 **Track 9**

TASKS

You are going to hear four voicemail messages.
There is one questions for each message.

214

- Look at the pictures and listen to the recording.
- You can note keywords below the pictures.
- Choose the correct picture and put a tick in the right box.
- You can listen to the recording twice.

Voicemail Message 1

1. Which shoes is the speaker recommending?

 *Boots*
 *Sneaker*
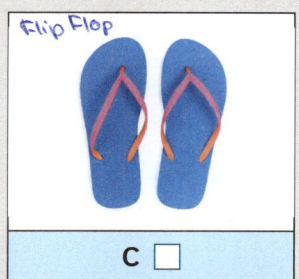 *Flip Flop*
 *heals High shoes*

| A ☐ | B ☐ | C ☐ | D ☒ ✓ |

_____

_____

_____

Voicemail Message 2

2. Which picture is the speaker reacting to?

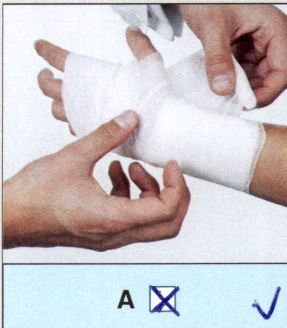

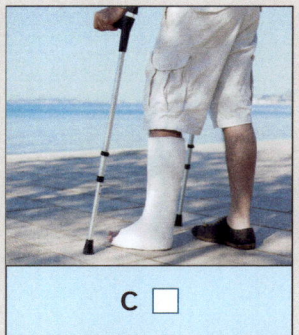

| A ☒ ✓ | B ☒ | C ☐ | D ☐ |

_____

_____

_____

_____

Voicemail Message 3

3. Which picture did the speaker send by mistake?

A ☐

B ☐

C ☒ ✓

D ☒

_____

_____

_____

_____

Voicemail Message 4

4. Which of these things does the speaker tell Zoe to bring?

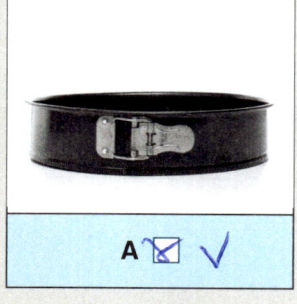

A ☒ ✓

B ☐

C ☒

D ☒

_____

_____

_____

_____

Listening Part 2: Radio Spots

 **Track 10**

You are going to hear four radio spots.
Note: You do not need to understand every word to do this task.

1/4

- You are going to hear four radio ads.
- Read the slogans below first, then listen to the recording.
- For each ad choose the correct slogan from the list (A–F). Put a tick in the right box of the grid below.
- There is only one slogan for each ad. Two slogans cannot be matched.
- You can listen to the recording twice.

A) Take care of all creatures great and small.

B) Clean up after your dog on the beach. — *Hund sauber machen, nach dem Strand*

C) Learn to speak with the world. — *Lerne mit der Welt zusprechen*

D) Protect yourself – don't let the sun shine down on you.

E) Take responsibility for your local beauty spot.

F) Want to travel the world and earn money?
   Then apply to teach English at one of our many language schools.

Number	Radio Spot	Slogan					
		A	B	C	D	E	F
5	Radio Spot 1				X			✓
6	Radio Spot 2			X ✓			X f
7	Radio Spot 3	X f				X	
8	Radio Spot 4		X f			X	

61

Listening Part 3: A Travel Podcast – Welkommen to Berlin

 **Track 11**

TASKS

- You are going to hear a travel podcast about a place called Berlin.
- You can listen to the recording twice.
- Complete the table below using keywords.

4/9

---

where it is:

9. ~~in Berlin~~ in a Country *f*

---

population:

10. ~~100 years~~ ~~and~~ 118 people 18tausend peaplee *f*

---

transport options in Berlin:

11. ~~Horst~~ buggy ✔

---

things to do/see for tourists (2):

12. ~~food,~~ bakery eat apple pie ✔

13. Horst on street *f*

Amish lifestyle:

14. freedom Asehalt *f*

---

why the Amish came to the US (2):

15. for freedom ✔

16. farmers ✔

---

how to get there:

17. ~~fly too~~ whut aboot *f*

---

*Listening Part 4: Taking Time Out

 Track 12

TASKS

You are going to hear part of a radio talk about taking a year out.
There are four people talking: a presenter, Katie, Sarah and Jacob.

4/8

- Read the statements below and listen to the recording.
- Put a tick in the box next to the correct statement.
- In each task only one statement is correct.
- You can listen to the recording twice.

18. This radio show is for young people who …	A	have just started studying at university.	☐
	B	are in their last year at school.	☒ ✓
	C	want to work with children.	☐

19. All three teenagers on this show …	A	spent time working abroad after school.	☒
	B	had a year without work after school.	☐
	C	had a year travelling around the world after school.	☒ ✗

20. Katie was an au pair …	A	and worked for a very old-fashioned family.	☐
	B	for a family with two small kids.	☒ ✓
	C	for an Australian family with a small child.	☐

21. During her time as an au pair, Katie felt …	A	like a slave because of all the housework.	☐
	B	she was treated like a family member by her host parents.	☒ ✓
	C	often lonely and bored.	☐

22. Jacob thinks that spending time abroad after school …	A	makes studying very hard when you come back.	☐
	B	makes you homesick and you miss your parents.	☒ ✗
	C	is a learning experience and helps you grow up.	☐

23. During his time in Australia …	A	Jacob needed a lot of money from his parents.	☐
	B	Jacob worked in different places.	☒ ✓
	C	Jacob had to go to hospital because of an accident.	☒

24.	A	cost almost nothing.	☐
Sarah's gap year as a volunteer in Mozambique ...	B	was altogether quite expensive.	☒ ✓
	C	was great because she earned £ 2,500.	☒

25.	A	that Katie got her driver's licence.	☒
Jacob was surprised to hear ...	B	that Katie got on so well with people and misses them.	☒ ✓
	C	that Katie's parents had to pay some money too.	☐

Teil II: Leseverstehen/Schreiben

Reading Part 1: Signs, Notices and Labels

TASKS

- Read the text of each sign/notice.
- Read the four statements next to it and decide which statement matches the sign.
- Tick the right statement. Only one of them is correct.

1.

Blackpool Pleasure Beach's "The Big One"

This ride is not suitable for elderly people, people with medical heart conditions and pregnant women.
Children under the age of 8 should be accompanied by a responsible adult.

A	Adults and children over 8 are not allowed on this ride.	☐
B	This attraction is suitable for elderly people.	☒
C	Elderly people and small children get a special discount on this ride.	☐
D	People with health problems and women who are expecting a child shouldn't go on this ride.	☐

2.

Tomco Express Supermarket

This fast checkout facility is for customers wishing to buy 6 items or fewer and will accept cash payment only.

A	You need a credit card at this check-out.	☐
B	You can use this checkout if you only buy very few things.	☐
C	You can only pay in cash if your total bill is under £ 6.	☒
D	This is a self-service checkout.	☐

3.

BELHAM INDOOR POOL
would like to inform its customers that this indoor pool will stay closed for its regular annual maintenance and repair work from July 1 to July 31.
We are looking forward to welcoming you back on August 1.

A	The pool is offering jobs to repair workers in July.	☐
B	They had an accident at the pool and need to repair it.	☐
C	The pool closes on August 1.	☒
D	The pool is not open in July.	☐

4.

WARNING!
(AUGUST TO DECEMBER):
Grey seal pupping beach ahead.

- Do not approach resting seals and keep all dogs on a lead.
- Do not allow dogs to bark at seals. Seals may abandon their pups and this beach if scared.
- Never put seals into water. They are on land for a reason.

Seals are legally protected under the Wildlife Act 1976. Help us keep them safe.

A	Dogs are not allowed at this beach.	☒
B	You must not let your dog run free or go near the seals.	☐
C	You should help to put seals back into water when you see them on land.	☐
D	You can only visit this beach from January to July.	☐

5.

Our library is a place of study and research. So please keep all noise in the reading rooms to a minimum. For users engaging in group work or needing to discuss their research we provide a special study area on the second floor.
Thank you.

A	Today there are many people studying in the library.	☐
B	Only the reading room on the 2nd floor is open today.	☐
C	You can talk to others or discuss your work on the 2nd floor.	☒
D	You're not allowed to talk anywhere in this library.	☐

Reading Part 2: Keeping Fit

TASKS

All the people below would like to do some kind of sports activity to stay fit.
- First read the information about them, then look at the different sports on the next page.
- Find two options/activities for each of the people below.
- Some activities can be chosen more than once.
- Write the letters of the activities in the boxes next to the right person.

No.	Activity 1	Activity 2		The persons
6/7	a	C		a) **Brenda** would like to do something for her general fitness but she isn't interested in weights or special muscle training. She doesn't want a regular course and prefers to train any time during the week. It's important for her to keep the weekends free. There could be months when she doesn't have much time, so she doesn't want to pay for membership every month.
8/9	e	F		b) **Angie** is a young student who would like regular physical exercise but doesn't have enough money to get a fitness club membership. She hates water sports. Last year she tried some Oriental things like yoga and tai chi but found them too slow and boring. Ideally she'd like to meet some new people while training once or twice a week. Angie can't pay more than £10 a month.
10/11	d	G		c) **Nick** thinks his body could look much better. He works in a bank all day so he would like a regular workout. He tried jogging but hated it. Nick would like better muscle definition or a "six- pack". He isn't really a team player and would prefer to train alone late in the evening or before he starts work. He is prepared to pay up to £50 a month.
12/13	e	F		d) **Jill** is in her early sixties. She would like to stay fit with some physical exercise – but nothing too stressful like jogging or weightlifting. The best thing would be a combination of exercise and wellness. She prefers indoor activities. Maybe some regular activity would also allow her to meet new people.
14/15	E	B		e) **Colin** used to be the goalkeeper in his college football team. Now he's got a full-time job and misses the exercise. For him a team sport would be ideal, but he doesn't mind other sports as long as he doesn't train alone or on machines. Colin has long and irregular working hours, so he only has time at weekends.

The activities

	**A)** New 24-hour indoor pool, Olympic size. Pay as you go, no membership required. Brand new sauna and steam bath facilities. Regular aqua fitness and baby swimming courses offered.
	**B)** Jazz dance course, Monday nights, £19.99/month, students pay half. Light exercise – a healthy and entertaining way to stay fit. Join us in the Odeon dance hall. Facilities include large dance floor, excellent music/loudspeaker system and air conditioning.
	**C)** 24-hour gym with sauna and modern equipment. Membership £39.99 a month. Meet new people and stay fit!
	**D)** Jogging club looking for new members. All levels welcome. No commitment, no fees. Just come when you want. We meet in Cheltenham Park every Sunday at 2 p.m.
	**E)** Five-a-side football needs new players. Sorry – men only. All ages welcome. No fees. Meet at University College Sports Hall on Sundays at 11 a.m. Please bring gym shoes.
	**F)** Learn tai chi with Ken Long from Shanghai. This old and gentle form of physical activity is suitable for all ages and all fitness levels. Meet in Victoria Park on Mondays (4 to 6 p.m.). One session costs £2. If you can't come, no problem: you won't need to pay.
	**G)** Rowing club needs money and invites non-members to use our training facilities. We have a wide range of high-tech machines – perfect for building up muscle strength, stamina and the perfect body. All the equipment is available from 8.30 p.m. to 11.30 p.m. from Monday to Friday. Facilities include showers and sauna. Cost is £25 per month.

*Reading Part 3: Mirror, Mirror on the Wall …

TASKS

- Read the text and the statements on the opposite page.
- Put a tick in the box next to the correct statement.
- For each task only one statement is correct.

Beauty contests or "beauty pageants", as they are often called, have a long tradition in the USA. Since the 1850s a variety of beauty contests for young women have been held regularly in small towns and big cities all over the States. There are various titles to compete for, for example the famous "Miss
5 America", who was first chosen in 1921.
The procedure is always similar – beautiful young women pose on stage in different outfits. They show off their bodies in swimsuits or ball gowns, they present their talents and do an interview in which they answer the jury's questions about popular culture, their future or family values. At the end the
10 jury decides and one of the girls can walk away with the crown as a beauty queen for one year. Often other prizes such as modeling or advertising contracts or even scholarships go along with the crown. Beauty queens are like American idols or role models: most American girls grow up with the dream of taking part in such a pageant and wearing a crown one day.
15 But even for a beauty queen, life isn't always without trouble, as was shown by 17-year-old Domonique Ramirez, Miss San Antonio 2011. After just a few weeks as a reigning queen, Miss Ramirez lost her crown and with it her title. The official organisers of the beauty contest decided to give both to Ashley Dixon, the girl who had come second in the original Miss San Antonio contest.
20 So what did Domonique Ramirez do wrong? There were no nude photos, no sex tapes and no alcohol or drug stories. The pageant directors claimed that Ramirez had turned up late for some events, wasn't a good representative of the city and allegedly they told her that she had put on too much weight. Linda Woods, a spokeswoman for the county's pageant board says that "as a Miss
25 San Antonio reigning queen, she has to live up to our rules and regulations". In an interview with a local radio station, Ms. Woods told the interviewer, "I said, you know, 'Get off the tacos, get off the chips and the soda.' Because she's 17, and that's what these kids eat".
Apparently, Miss Ramirez was doing a photo shoot in which she was asked
30 to wear a dress from the original beauty competition and it didn't fit her anymore. Miss Ramirez also claimed that after a bikini photo shoot she was told to lose at least 13 pounds. Ramirez is 5'8, (172 cm) and weighs 129 pounds (58 kg) – which is by no means overweight.
But Domonique Ramirez didn't give up. She wanted to fight for her crown,
35 so she took a lawyer and went to court. "This is about principle, this is about what's right", Ramirez said. Although San Antonio pageant officials say that their decision had nothing to do with Miss Ramirez' weight, judges didn't quite believe that. In March 2011 she won her court case and was given her crown and title back. So in 2011 for the first time ever, San Antonio, Texas, has two
40 reigning beauty queens: Domonique Ramirez and Ashley Dixon.

This story might show one of the less savoury sides of beauty contests and it certainly highlights the debate on healthy body images. However, one little story that recently went through the media is even more worrying: In the popular US reality show "Toddlers and Tiaras", a televised child beauty contest, a mother dressed up her four-year-old daughter as Dolly Parton – the country 45 singer who is not only famous for her music but also for her sizeable breasts. Of course, the little girl was wearing make-up – quite normal in shows like this –, but her mother went one step further and put extra padding into some parts of the girl's dress. This way her little 4-year-old girl looked just like Dolly Parton – with large boobs and a big bottom. The show attracted a lot 50 of worldwide criticism after its screening.

TASKS

16. The first American beauty contests ...	A	were held in the second half of the 19th century.	☐
	B	were organised in 1921.	☐
	C	were called "Miss America Pageants".	☒
	D	were only held in big cities.	☐

17. At most modern beauty pageants, ...	A	the girls are not allowed to speak.	☐
	B	a jury decides who wins the contest.	☒ ✓
	C	the girls don't need to pose in swimsuits.	☐
	D	both A + C	☐

18. Beauty queens ...	A	often win other prizes along with the crown.	☒
	B	are often idolised by little American girls.	☐
	C	can usually keep their crown for one year.	☐
	D	all of the above (A + B + C)	☐

19. Ashley Dixon ...	A	won the original Miss San Antonio Beauty Pageant 2011.	☐
	B	lost her crown after a few weeks but got it back.	☐
	C	came second in the original competition.	☒ ✓
	D	works as a director on the San Antonio Pageant Board.	☐

20. Miss Ramirez thinks she lost her title ...	A	because she had alcohol problems.	☐
	B	because of some old photos of her naked.	☒
	C	because she wasn't thin enough.	☐
	D	both A + B	☐

69

21.	A	Domonique Ramirez didn't want to be naked.	☐
In one photo session ...	B	a dress from the competition was too small for Miss Ramirez.	☒
	C	she was told to lose some weight.	☐
	D	both B + C	☐

22.	A	she lost 13 pounds.	☐
Miss Ramirez won her crown back because ...	B	she competed in a new contest and won it.	☒
	C	she talked to the directors and they agreed on new regulations together.	☐
	D	she hired a lawyer and went to court.	☐

23.	A	that San Antonio, Texas, had a beauty pageant.	☐
2011 was the first time ever ...	B	that there were two reigning beauty queens in San Antonio.	☐
	C	that a Latina became "Miss San Antonio".	☐
	D	that a beauty queen went on to study law.	☒

24.	A	a mother used make up on her little daughter.	☒
In the child beauty contest "Toddlers and Tiaras", ...	B	a mother dressed up her daughter (aged 4) as Dolly Parton, using fake breasts and bottom padding.	☐
	C	Dolly Parton criticised the mother of a 4-year-old.	☐
	D	both A + B	☐

25.	A	there are so many reality shows on US television.	☐
The author finds it worrying that ...	B	that many people criticised the reality show with a "Mini Dolly Parton".	☒
	C	a mother sees nothing wrong with dressing up her 4-year-old daughter like that.	☐
	D	both B + C	☐

Writing Part 1: Your Photo

TASKS

You have posted this photo online. Your friend Sarah wants to know more about it.

- React to her comment and answer the questions.
- Write 40–50 words.

Cool make-up!
Where was this
picture taken?
Who are these two?
Why are they
dressed like that?
How did other people
react?

Thank you, the picture where an
Halloween ~~os~~ in ~~s~~ the clueb in New York.
~~It~~ The two people are my friend and
me, we ~~would~~ wore a ~~partner~~ matching Halloween
Castum costume, the orther people's reaction
was ~~of~~ at first wierd than scary, but
funny. We ~~wish~~ hope you had a great
Halloween party.

Best wishes.

/ 5 P.

Writing Part 2: A Camping Trip with Friends

TASKS

You have found this message posted on the internet.

- Write a letter to Ian and answer his questions.
- Write between 100–160 words.
- Do not use internet slang.

Hi there,
I'm quite angry at the moment. My parents are impossible! I'm 15 years old and they won't allow me to go on holiday with my friends! Some of my classmates want to go camping in Spain for a week and my parents just say "No". They say there's not enough money and they think I'm too young to go abroad without them. I can have a week in the Welsh mountains together with them! That's just so boring! Is this normal? What do you think? Are you allowed to go on holiday without your parents? What can I do to convince my parents to let me go? How could I get some extra holiday money? All ideas are welcome!
Thanks, Ian

Hi Ian, That's bad to hear.
Your parents say "No" to going on holiday with your friend, I understand your parents because you 15 years old and they are coorried about your ask, but you can your parents of what your friend in the holiday come too.
that would be more funny in the mountains, it is not the same but a solution. and next year your will be 16 years old and have more responsibities of your self and than your go with your friend apan Spain.
I could that extra money is not where thankfull is what why way your of the money and seller the time whit your parents and maybe your friend.

Best wishes
your Agony Aunt

Inhalt:	/ 6 P.	Sprache:	/ 6 P.	Gesamt:	/ 12 P.

⋆ Writing Part 3: Mediation – Young German Talents

TASKS

Your English-speaking friend Kim is doing a project about young talents in other European countries.
She wants to hear your ideas for a young German talent.

- Read the two online profiles on the following page.
- Choose **one** profile.
- Write an email to Kim and tell her about your chosen talent.
- Say what the person you chose does and mention at least four aspects of their career.
- Do not translate word for word.
- Write complete sentences.

Dear Kim,

Tarin Wilda is so a talent in person, she styled 2017 are 16-paece for H und M, ~~whit~~ ~~If~~ ~~she~~ ~~was~~ She was also a guest at cro, her ~~tied~~ song "Bist du daon,, was 2017 ~~realeest~~ published. in spite of German-Lyrics is her song popular so that in USA and Kanada a hit is and the magazine Vogue that published. She as a training to Hair-Stylisten and passion as model.

Thats it.

Best wishes
Samantha Fleck

Inhalt:	/ 4 P.	Sprache:	/ 4 P.	Gesamt:	/ 8 P.

Ace Tee (Rapperin/R&B-Musikerin)

Jenfeld auf. Ihre Eltern stammen aus Ghana. Nach einem abgebrochenen Besuch der Akademie POP im Hamburg machte sie eine Ausbildung zur Hairstylistin. Daneben begann sie unter dem Künstlernamen *MEDUZV* Musik zu machen.

Im Jahr 2016 veröffentlichte Ace Tee ihr Lied *Bist du down*, das sie mit dem 21-jährigen Rapper *Kwam.e* aufgenommen hatte. Das Video dazu drehte sie in Eigenregie unter einer Eisenbahnbrücke in Hamburg-Altona-Nord. Der Clip machte sie dann über die Grenzen Deutschlands hinaus bekannt: Eine X-Nutzerin aus Kanada war davon so begeistert, dass sie das Video verbreitete und Ace Tee mit berühmten Musikerinnen der 90er-Jahre wie TLC und Aaliyah verglich. Der Clip wurde trotz der deutschsprachigen Lyrics so populär, dass selbst die Modezeitschrift *Vogue* darüber berichtete. Das hatte sicherlich damit zu tun, dass Ace Tee außer der Musik auch eine Leidenschaft für Mode hat. Im Video zu *Bist du down* trägt sie mehr als zehn verschiedene Outfits. In einem Interview mit der *ZEIT* sagte sie sinngemäß, wie wichtig es ist, dass man authentisch zeige, wie man ist und wie man sich fühlt – auch durch Kleidung. Man könne auch mit einer Jogginghose im Club tanzen oder mit einer breiten Zahnlücke rumlaufen. Das sei ihr Credo.

Für H&M hat sie 2017 eine 16-teilige Modekollektion entworfen, bei Cro war sie Gastmusikerin, und ihr Lied *Bist du down* wurde selbst in den USA und Kanada zum Hit. Ihre erste EP *Tee Time* erschien im September 2017.

Ace Tees bürgerlicher Name ist Tarin Wilda. Sie wurde 1993 in Berlin geboren und wuchs dann im Hamburger Stadtteil

Edin Hasanović (Schauspieler)

Seine Mutter flüchtete mit ihm als Baby vor dem Krieg in Bosnien-Herzegowina nach Berlin. Hier wuchs Edin Hasanović auf. Als Kind liebte er es, Leute nachzuahmen und schon mit sieben Jahren probte er eine Oscarrede vor seiner Familie.

Inzwischen ist der 1992 geborene Edin Hasanović einer der erfolgreichsten Jungschauspieler Deutschlands. Mit 13 nahm er an mehreren Castings teil und stand kurz danach auf der Bühne des Berliner Ensembles. Dort arbeitete er zwei Jahre lang als Schauspieler, bevor er mit nur 15 Jahren eine Rolle in der Fernsehserie „KDD – Kriminaldauerdienst" erhielt, in der er von 2007–2010 mitspielte. Trotz Theaterarbeit und Fernsehdreharbeiten fand Edin genug Zeit zum Lernen und legte 2011 sein Abitur an der Heinz-Schliemann-Schule in Berlin-Prenzlauer Berg ab. Wie er Schule und Filmen vereinbaren konnte? Neben eigener Arbeit und Selbstdisziplin unterstützten ihn seine Lehrer/-innen und die Filmemacher/-innen, indem sie z. B. Dreh- und Klausurtermine aufeinander abstimmten.

Inzwischen ist Edin Hasanović dem deutschen Publikum auch durch Hauptrollen in verschiedenen Filmen wie „Im Westen nichts Neues" und „Je suis Karl" bekannt. Für seine Rolle in „Schuld sind immer die Anderen" erhielt er 2016 den Filmpreis Goldene Kamera als bester deutscher Nachwuchsschauspieler. Es folgten weitere Nominierungen und Preise. Unter anderem wurde die deutsche Dramedy-Miniserie „Familie Braun", in der Edin Hasanović einen Neonazi verkörpert, der mit einer Afrikanerin ein Kind zeugt, im November 2017 sogar als internationale Produktion mit dem bekannten US-Fernsehpreis Emmy ausgezeichnet. Sicherlich bleibt dies nicht der letzte Preis für den jungen Schauspieler, der schon an weiteren Filmprojekten arbeitet.

Schriftliche Prüfungsarbeit zur erweiterten Berufsbildungsreife und zum Mittleren Schulabschluss im Fach Englisch 2023

Quelle der Aufgabenstellung

Lisum Landesinstitut für Schule und Medien Berlin-Brandenburg

Aus lizenzrechtlichen Gründen weichen alle Abbildungen sowie die Materialtexte „Listening Part 2: Radio Ads 1+2", „Listening Part 3: Board Games from Around the World", „Reading Part 1: A–G" und „Reading Part 2: Short Texts 11–16" von der Darstellung in der Original-Prüfungsarbeit ab.

Bei den Musterlösungen handelt es sich um nicht amtliche Lösungen.

INFO

Im Jahr 2023 bestand die schriftliche Prüfungsarbeit in Berlin wie in Brandenburg lediglich aus den beiden Bereichen Hörverstehen und Leseverstehen.

Teil I: Hörverstehen

Listening Part 1: Voicemail Messages

_____ /4 P  Track 13

AUFGABEN

- You are going to hear four people reacting to pictures which were sent in an online chat.
- You will hear the recording twice.
- Look at the pictures and then listen to each message.
- Decide which picture each speaker reacts to and put a tick in the right box.

Message One

1. Which picture does the speaker react to?

Message Two

2. Which picture does the speaker react to?

Message Three

3. Which picture does the speaker react to?

Listening Part 2: Radio Ads

_____1_____ /4 P 🎧 Track 14

AUFGABEN

Please note: You do not need to understand every word to do this task.

- You are going to hear four radio ads.
- You will hear the recording twice.
- Read the slogans below first, then listen to the recording.
- For each ad choose the correct slogan from the list (A–F) and put a tick in the right box.
- There is only one correct slogan for each ad.
- Two slogans can't be matched.

A) **Take time out**

B) **Report crimes to help the police**

C) **Don't let strangers see your valuables**

D) **Not all devices belong in the garbage**

E) **Don't let food go to waste**

F) **Put a rainbow on your plate**

Number	Radio Ads	A	B	C	D	E	F
5	Radio Ad 1	✗			✗		✗
6	Radio Ad 2		✗			✗	✗
7*	Radio Ad 3		✗	✗			
8	Radio Ad 4	✗		✗			

Listening Part 3: Board Games from Around the World

 _5_ /9 P Track 15

- You are going to hear three people talking about popular games played around the world.
- You will hear the recording twice.
- Complete the table below. Use 1 to 5 words or numbers for each answer.

	Type of board game	How speaker got to know the game	How to win the game	What speaker likes
Lotería	9 Bingo ✓	search engine celebrating game	10 4 picture of a line ✓	11 after match... learn spanish ✓
Senet	12 strategy game	13 Museum ✓	14* all your pices on your board ✓	
Carrom	15* ✗	16 must Familie in café ✓	score 25 points	17 ability konzentauten ✓

Listening Part 4: How Woke Are You?

_2_ /8 P  Track 16

AUFGABEN

- You are going to hear the first part of a live podcast.
- There are four speakers: the hosts Jamila J. and Kendrick Hill and the callers Jason and Riz.
- You will hear the recording twice.
- Read the statements below first, then listen to the recording.
- Put a tick in the box next to the correct statement.
- Only one statement is correct in each case.

18.* What is said about the phrase "stay woke"?	A	It was brought to the US by immigrants.	☒
	B	It is used by white people to discriminate against minorities.	☐
	C	Its meaning has expanded over the years.	☐

19.* Jamila says that people who are "woke"	A	have experienced some form of racism in their life.	☒
	B	take part in political demonstrations.	☐
	C	avoid stereotyping when communicating.	☐

20.* How does Jamila feel about wokeness?	A	She is unsure about how to behave in certain situations.	☐
	B	She is worried that it will divide society.	☒
	C	both A + B	☐

21.* What did social media users criticise about the film that Kendrick watched?	A	The message of the film was unclear.	☐
	B	The choice of actors was not suitable.	☐
	C	The film was too political.	☒

22.* What did Jamila say about the evening she spent playing cards with her friends?	A	They didn't use a traditional deck of cards.	☒
	B	They got into a heated debate.	☐
	C	both A + B	☒

23. * What's Jason's opinion on woke culture?	A	People have other priorities.	☐
	B	He would like to see more research.	☐
	C	It excludes white men like him.	☒

24. Riz advises Jason to	A	stop feeling guilty about being white.	☐
	B	join a group of activists.	☐
	C	think about the way he speaks.	☒

25. * How will the podcast be improved?	A	There will be a new interactive app for the listeners.	☐
	B	The podcast will be made accessible to more people.	☒
	C	Listeners can suggest topics for the next episode.	☐

Teil II: Leseverstehen

Reading Part 1: What to Do in and Around Boston (USA)

6 / 10 P.

- These people are looking for something to do in and around Boston.
- First read the information about the people, then look at the descriptions of things to do (A–G) on the following two pages.
- In each case find the **two** activities the people would do. Write the letters of the activities in the boxes next to the people's names.
- Some of the activities can be chosen more than once.

No.	Activity 1	Activity 2		The people
1/2	A	D ✓		**Vanessa** loves the seaside location of Boston. That's why she would like to see the city from there. Enjoying a great nightly sightseeing trip would be a perfect start for her weekend trip. But she is also here for the rich cultural heritage of the East Coast. Since she doesn't have much time, she would take a tour that offers as many different places of cultural interest as possible in one day.
3/4	B / E	G / B		**Ethan's** kids have already warned him that they won't go on another one of these guided sightseeing bus tours. Instead they want to be active. So he needs an activity that is fun and allows his family to get away from the crowds. If his partner takes the kids, he would also love to do something on his own. It would be great to improve his photography skills with the help of a professional for example.
5/6	C / D	E / C		**Aubrey's** motto is: pics or it didn't happen. So she wants to go on a tour that helps her remember Boston through the lens of her camera – with her in the center. And later perhaps she can even upload pictures of some hidden places. Exploring Boston at night could also be interesting. She is looking for a tour where she can hear stories about the mysterious side of the city.
7/8	E / B	F / E		For **Kayla** getting to know a city starts with learning about its past. She would love to go on a tour offering exactly that but which is also interesting for her two younger children. For a second tour, she would like to treat herself to a whole day full of good food and beautiful sights which she can take pictures of. She hopes her followers will "like" them.

9/10	A F	G A		**Alessandro** and his soccer team are in Boston for the first time. First and foremost they want to experience the athletic and fun part of the city. So for a start they think of any activity that could prove a physical challenge for them. Later there should be no holding back on the dance floor if there is any tour that fits.

Boston Odyssey Dinner Tour 	**A)** Whether you want to impress someone special or you are looking for a good night out with friends, this three-hour tour around Boston Harbor offers you a fantastic experience with a difference. Feast on a three-course dinner aboard while enjoying a sunset view of the Boston skyline. You can enjoy looking at illuminated landmarks, eating great food and walking on deck under the stars or you can enjoy the beats in the ship's nightclub where you can hit the dance floor and have fun with great music and our live entertainment. *Speziale / Besondere nacht mit deinem Freund, Eine Tour die 3 std durch Boston geht*
Photography Walking Tour 	**B)** This leisurely walk will take you to a very special neighborhood of Boston – Beacon Hill. Our experienced professional photographer guide will lead you to the key landmarks through a maze of small streets and alleyways. Listen to the historical commentary on the houses while learning how to capture incredible photos with the camera or phone of your choice. No prior experience is necessary, and our guide will share their expert knowledge and tricks of how to get great images from the best angle. *– besondere Nachbarschaft.* *– profi Photograf als guide* *↳ bringt dir bei was du mit deiner camera oder Handy besser machen kannst.*
Ghost and Gravestone Tour 	**C)** This slightly different evening tour takes you to the city's dark sides and haunted places. You can hop onto "the Trolley of the Doomed" and our aptly costumed guide will lead you on a journey into the dark and spooky history of the city. You will be taken to two of the city's oldest burial grounds where you will be told about the intriguing and gruesome past of the city. Historical information mixed with local ghost tales guarantee you an exciting evening. As some stories can contain details of murder and violence, parental guidance for children under 13 is strongly recommended. *– schlechte seite von Boston*
Museums Tour 	**D)** This all-day experience will allow you to see the best museums, art and culture in the Boston area with the comfort of personal transportation, your own tour guide and photographer. Your first stop will be Stockbridge, Massachusetts, which is where the famous painter Norman Rockwell found the setting for many of his masterpieces. Then the tour will take you to Springfield, Massachusetts, where more amazing locations are waiting for you: an American novelist's museum, a botanical garden, a sculptor's exhibition and the house and museum of Mark Twain, the famous creator of Tom Sawyer and Huckleberry Finn. *– Museum mit Profi Photograf*

Boston Selfie Tour	**E)** If you are interested in sights, history and fantastic food, combined with the opportunity of capturing this experience in amazing pictures – for your friends to see and for yourself to remember – then this is the adventure for you. Our local guides will pick you up from your hotel in the morning. In a spacious, comfortable and, of course, air-conditioned vehicle you will be taken to the most "Instagrammable" locations Boston has to offer – famous landmarks, historical buildings, exciting secret locations and more will make this full-day tour unforgettable. *Sehenswürdigkeit Profi photograph*

Boston Tea Party Tour	**F)** On this tour a historical event is brought to life for you. In a floating museum you can see authentically restored tea ships, enjoy hi-tech interactive exhibits and the performance of live actors. With all your senses you will become part of the events of the night of December 16, 1773, when the Sons of Liberty threw tea overboard which subsequently led to the independence of the USA from Britain. Unforgettable, entertaining and educational for children of all ages and adults alike. *– Museum + tea*

Skyline and Sunset Kayak Tour	**G)** Looking for a leisurely but active way to spend the day in the Boston area? Why not rent a kayak or canoe and have a day on the Charles River? You can take friends or family, and kids are allowed to operate their own boat from the age of eight. Our guided group and individual tours start from the river banks of the Charles so you can take in the amazing views of Boston and Cambridge from the water. We also offer lessons for those who want to advance their canoeing or kayaking skills. *Kayak tour durch Boston*

Reading Part 2: Short Texts

/ 6 P.

AUFGABEN

- Look at the text and the statements in each task.
- What does the text say?
- Put a tick next to the statement that matches the text – **A, B, C** or **D.**
- There is only one correct statement for each sign.

11

POOL CAPACITY

MAXIMUM NUMBERS OF SWIMMERS/BATHERS ALLOWED IN THIS POOL AT ANY ONE TIME: **12**

Opening hours: 10 am to 6 pm Use of the pool is prohibited outside these hours.

Which of the following is allowed?

A	five swimmers at 11 in the morning	☐
B	pool party at 8 o'clock	☒
C	seven bathers at 10 in the evening	☐
D	14 swimmers at 1 in the afternoon	☒

12

Hi Jenna! Just a friendly reminder of your phone interview tomorrow with Hi5 Networks at 11 AM. If you need some last-minute help with prep, just reply to this message and we can figure out a time to chat right away. If I don't hear from you, good luck! I know you're going to do great. ☺

Marco L. at Seattle Staffing – Reply STOP at any time to unsubscribe

The person who wrote this note

A	is looking for a job.	☐
B	is accepting an invitation.	☐
C	is asking for an appointment.	☐
D	is offering assistance.	☒

13

DiscountDay

Luxury Chocolate Cream Cookies

DiscountDays UK is recalling
Luxury Chocolate Cream Cookies, 176 g, £ 0.89
Best-before dates: 30.05.2024 to 17.08.2024

Product may contain small traces of hazelnuts and pea-nuts, which are not declared in English on the packaging. This means there is a possible health risk to anyone with an allergy to nuts.

If you have bought the product and have a nut allergy, do not eat it. Instead, return it to any **DiscountDays UK** store for a full refund. Other or similar products with different best-before dates are not affected.

DiscountDays UK apologises to all customers for any in-convenience caused.

The product shown in the picture

A	is on special offer.	☐
B	is available for a limited time.	☐
C	has a new, improved recipe.	☒
D	may harm some consumers.	☐

14*

TO THE PERSON WHO USES
A SPONGE TO CLEAN
THEIR PORRIDGE BOWL
EVERY DAY: <u>PLEASE STOP</u>.
USE THE BRUSH INSTEAD.

We're going through
sponges quicker than we
can purchase them.

– Management –

This note tells the reader how to

A	save water.	☒
B	make porridge.	☐
C	wash the dishes.	☐
D	load the dishwasher.	☐

15

Due to repeated vandalism and theft of its contents, this vending machine will remain empty until it can undergo repair as well as be securely protected from future abuse.

We would like to apologise to those of you who have been using the machine correctly and with honest intention.

Thank you for your understanding.

This machine is empty because

A	its products are sold out.	☐
B	it needs cleaning.	☐
C	it has been misused.	☑
D	it will be moved.	☐

✓

16 *

Tanitoluwa Adewumi captured people's hearts worldwide when in 2019, at the age of 8, he won the New York State Scholastic Chess Championship. Remarkably, Tanitoluwa, known as Tani, had only been playing chess for a year at this time. He was living with his parents in a homeless shelter in Manhattan after they had to emigrate from Nigeria following the Boko Haram terror attacks. A GoFundMe page was set up by his coaches to support Tani's development and within a short time it raised over $ 250,000. Two years later, in 2021, Tani was the 28th youngest player to become a US National Master. While continuing to be very successful at chess, the young prodigy has written a book and started a foundation to raise awareness and support for the situation of refugees and homeless people.

The boy Tani

A	was awarded an important title in chess.	☐
B	won $ 250,000 in a chess tournament.	☐
C	is the youngest chess world champion ever.	☑
D	teaches refugees how to play chess.	☐

Reading Part 3: Britain's Problem with Pets

AUFGABEN

- Read the text and the statements on the following two pages.
- Put a tick in the box next to the correct answer.
- Only one answer is correct in each case.

Henrietta Morrison confidently plunges her spoon into a tin of slow-cooked lamb hotpot and lifts out a mouthful for inspection. She passes her nostrils over the meat chunks and accompanying sauce, smiles, then places the whole lot into her mouth. "Delicious," she remarks, as a small crowd of onlookers
5 gathers round to watch the spectacle.
[…]
Morrison has a point to prove, though: she is at Europe's largest pet trade show, PetIndex, at the Birmingham NEC, and her company, Lily's Kitchen, sells the most expensive pet food on the market. Her dog food, for example,
10 retails in places such as Harrods for more than £2 a tin, with the promise that the contents are "proper food". […] But now the industry faces a new source of criticism: just what is the environmental impact of feeding the huge quantity of "companion" animals around the world?
A new book with the somewhat provocative title of *Time to Eat the Dog? The*
15 *Real Guide to Sustainable Living* has triggered a highly charged debate about the environmental efficacy of our pet-owning habits. […] "According to the authors … it takes 0.84 hectares [2.07 acres] of land to keep a medium-sized dog fed. In contrast, running a 4.6-litre Toyota Land Cruiser, including the energy required to construct the thing and drive it 10,000 km a year, requires
20 0.41 hectares. Dogs are not the only environmental sinners. The eco-footprint of a cat equates to that of a Volkswagen Golf. If that's troubling, there is an even more shocking comparison. In 2004, the average citizen of Vietnam had an ecological footprint of 0.76 hectares. For an Ethiopian, it was just 0.67 hectares. In a world where scarce resources are already hogged by the rich,
25 can we really justify keeping pets that take more than some people?" […]
Michael Bellingham, the chief executive of the Pet Food Manufacturer's Association, argues that the benefits of pets need to be viewed more holistically, rather than just through the prism of their "carbon pawprint". "Our environment, far from being threatened by pets, is greatly enriched by the part they
30 play in our lives," he says. "Pets in the home instill responsibility, encourage social as well as environmental awareness and have positive health benefits on children. Furthermore, children from households with pets are found to have stronger immune systems and take fewer days off school. People with pets make fewer visits to the doctor – 21% less for elderly people. What large
35 polluting car improves your health and gets you out for a walk every day?"
[…] That we greatly benefit from the presence of pets isn't really disputed. But in order to reduce their impact on the environment, should there possibly be a limit to the number of pets we have? Because, of course, it's not just the food they eat that's the problem. Some conservationists, for example, have
40 long been saying that the population of domesticated cats is having a harmful

impact on native fauna. As meat eaters, cats are, by instinct, opportunistic hunters. A 2005 study in Bristol, for example, showed that 131 cats returned home 358 animals – birds, small mammals and amphibians – over the course of a year. It didn't record the prey the cats failed to return home. [...] But dogs aren't exactly guilt-free, given that an estimated 250,000 tonnes of dog faeces are deposited on our streets and in our parks each year. [...] 45

Anyone who owns a pet will keenly testify how much joy and companionship they can bring. But they will also acknowledge just how much time, effort and money they can require, too: a tortoise needs its heat and lighting; a horse needs shoeing and a regular supply of straw; an iguana needs its supply of insects; a chicken needs grit and corn; a dog needs its delousing powder; a cat needs a scratch tower. And then there's the insurance, the vet's fees and the annual cost of food and bedding. It's little wonder that some pets are described as being as big a commitment as having a child in the home. So it shouldn't really come as a surprise that some are now viewing pets as having a similar environmental impact to that of a small person. After all, in many owners' eyes, their pets are very much part of the family. 50 55

Leo Hickman, "Britain's problem with pets: they're bad for the planet", in: *The Guardian*, London, 13 November 2009, https://www.theguardian.com/environment/2009/nov/13/ethical-living-carbon-emissions (accessed on 8 August 2023, adapted)
Copyright Guardian News & Media Ltd 2023

Reading Part 3: Britain's Problem with Pets   / 9 P.

17. What is Henrietta doing at the pet trade show?	A	Feeding her dog on stage	☐
	B	Watching dogs performing tricks	☐
	C	Promoting her own brand of dog food	☒
	D	Giving tips on dog training	☐

18.* What is the pet food industry being criticised for?	A	Animals are abused for pet food commercials.	☐
	B	Premium pet food is not sold in supermarkets.	☒
	C	The quality of pet food is not always guaranteed.	☐
	D	The production of pet food could be bad for the planet.	☐

19.* In the book *Time to Eat the Dog?* it is stated that	A	eating dog meat can harm human health.	☐
	B	dogs need large outdoor spaces to run around in.	☐
	C	some dogs are worse for the planet than a big car.	☐
	D	both A + B	☒

20.* The book also states that	A	pet cats need a safe environment to live in.	☒
	B	the most environmentally friendly cars come from Asia.	☐
	C	a pet can have a higher carbon footprint than a person.	☐
	D	many people have become aware of their carbon footprint.	☐

21.* Michael Bellingham points out that	A	there are significant advantages to having a pet.	☐
	B	pets can cause allergies in children.	☐
	C	a lot of people treat their pets like human beings.	☐
	D	pets are more and more affected by pollution.	☒

22.* Which idea(s) does the author put forward to deal with the problems of keeping pets?	A	Feed pets vegetarian food	☐
	B	Have fewer pets	☐
	C	Choose a small pet	☐
	D	all of them (A + B + C)	☒

23.* What is said about cats as pets?	A	They should be allowed to roam freely outside.	☒
	B	They endanger local wildlife.	☐
	C	They are choosy eaters.	☐
	D	Their poo can harm other animals' health.	☐

24.* Pet owners admit that their pets	A	need a lot of care.	☐
	B	have a carbon footprint comparable to a child's.	☐
	C	are treated as family members.	☒
	D	all of them (A + B + C)	☐

25.* The focus of the text is on	A	dealing with the overpopulation of pets.	☒
	B	exploring attitudes of pet owners.	☐
	C	research on the environmental impact of pets.	☐
	D	companies' attempts to sell luxurious pet products.	☐

Teil B Die mündliche Prüfung

B 1 Berlin: Vorbereitung – Let's get ready for the oral test!

B 1.1 Berlin: Was wird in der mündlichen Prüfung erwartet?

Bei der Überprüfung der mündlichen Sprechfertigkeit handelt es sich um eine **Partnerprüfung** von maximal 15 Minuten Dauer. Sie erfolgt **ohne Vorbereitungszeit.**

Das Prüfungsgespräch führt dein Englischlehrer beziehungsweise deine Englischlehrerin. Außerdem wird eine zweite Fachkraft anwesend sein. Diese Lehrkraft beobachtet die Prüfung und fertigt ein Protokoll an. Sie beteiligt sich aber nicht aktiv an der Prüfung.

Das mündliche Prüfungsgespräch besteht aus **vier Teilen**. Überprüft wird deine Fähigkeit, sprachlich korrekt auf verschiedene Gesprächs- oder Bildimpulse zu reagieren, deine Meinung überzeugend auszudrücken und dabei angemessen auf eine/-n Gesprächspartner/-in einzugehen.

B 1.2 Berlin: Zum Aufbau der mündlichen Prüfung (Partnerprüfung)

Die mündliche Prüfung setzt sich aus **vier Teilen** zusammen, in denen deine mündliche Sprechfertigkeit auf unterschiedliche Weise überprüft wird:

Teil 1 (ca. 2–3 Minuten): Die prüfende Lehrkraft begrüßt deine/-n Partner/-in und dich. Sie stellt euch abwechselnd Fragen zur Person, zu Hobbys und Freizeitaktivitäten, Vorlieben beziehungsweise Abneigungen und ähnlichen Themen. In der Regel werdet ihr auch aufgefordert, ein englisches Wort zu buchstabieren.

Teil 2 (ca. 2–3 Minuten): Der/Die Prüfende schildert euch eine Situation (z. B. die gemeinsame Urlaubsplanung) und fordert euch auf, passende Vorschläge zu unterbreiten, zu diskutieren und eine Entscheidung herbeizuführen. Unterstützend erhaltet ihr Bilder, über die ihr sprechen könnt.

Teil 3 (ca. 3 Minuten): Nacheinander erhaltet ihr nun ein Bild, das ihr eurer Partnerin bzw. eurem Partner etwa eine Minute zusammenhängend und in sinnvoller Reihenfolge beschreiben sollt.

Teil 4 (ca. 3 Minuten): Die Bilder aus Teil 3 sollen nun von euch zum Anlass genommen werden, ein Thema gemeinsam zu diskutieren. Hier geht es darum, Argumente zu entwickeln und die eigene Meinung überzeugend auszudrücken.

INFO zum Prüfungsablauf

Die Überprüfung der mündlichen Sprechfertigkeit erfolgt in vier Teilen:

1. **Kontakt aufnehmen:** Small Talk
2. **Etwas aushandeln:** Partnergespräch
3. **Ein Bild beschreiben:** zusammenhängend sprechen
4. **Über ein Thema diskutieren:** Partnergespräch

Prüfungsteil	Mögliche Themen und Inhalte	Übungshinweise
PT 1: Kontakt aufnehmen	– Fragen beantworten zu Person, Familie, Schule, Haustieren, Vorlieben, Hobbys, zur Art der Prüfungsvorbereitung, zum Berufswunsch – Buchstabieren	Tipps und Übungen zu diesem Prüfungsteil findest du auf S. 93–95
PT 2: Etwas aushandeln	– Planung einer Urlaubsreise, Klassen- oder Auslandsfahrt – Auswahl eines Geburtstagsgeschenkes oder eines Mitbringsels – Organisation eines Picknicks, einer Schulveranstaltung, eines Projekttages – Planung von Freizeitaktivitäten, Festen und Feiern	Tipps und Übungen zu diesem Prüfungsteil findest du auf S. 96–97

PT 3: Ein Bild beschreiben	Bilder, die Anlass zu einem Gespräch geben, z. B. – eine belebte Straßenszene, eine dörfliche Idylle, ein Restaurant oder Straßencafé, eine Bahnhofshalle oder Hotellobby; oder – Menschen, die Sport treiben, essen, lesen, spielen, arbeiten usw.	Tipps und Übungen zu diesem Prüfungsteil findest du auf S. 97–99
PT 4: Über ein Thema diskutieren	Diskussionen über gesunde Ernährung und Essgewohnheiten, soziales Engagement, Umwelt, gesunde Lebensweise, sinnvolle Freizeitbeschäftigung usw.	Tipps und Übungen zu diesem Prüfungsteil findest du auf S. 100–101

B 1.3 Berlin: Kriterien der Bewertung

Die prüfende Lehrkraft und die/der Protokollführende nehmen unmittelbar nach der Prüfung die Bewertung deiner Sprechleistung vor. Dabei stehen vier Bewertungskriterien im Mittelpunkt, die gleichwertig in die Endbeurteilung deiner Leistung einfließen:
– die kommunikative Kompetenz,
– der Gesprächsbeitrag,
– Grammatik und Wortschatz, und
– die Aussprache.

Kommunikative Kompetenz	Gesprächsbeitrag	Grammatik und Wortschatz	Aussprache
– Gelingt es dir, Gespräche zu eröffnen, fortzuführen und zu beenden?	– Kannst du deine Gedanken sinnvoll strukturieren und ausdrücken?	– Gelingt es dir, grammatische Strukturen möglichst fehlerfrei zu verwenden (z. B. bei der Fragebildung und den Zeitformen)?	– Sind deine Aussprache und Intonation so gut, dass man dich problemlos versteht?
– Sprichst du verständlich und in vollständigen Sätzen?	– Sprichst du zum Thema?	– Verfügst du über einen Wortschatz, der es dir ermöglicht, viele Themen spontan und verständlich zu diskutieren?	– Sprichst du flüssig?
– Stellst du verständliche Fragen und gehst auf die Äußerungen deiner Partnerin bzw. deines Partners ein?	– Gehst du auf deine Partnerin / deinen Partner ein?		

B 1.4 Berlin: Tipps zur Vorbereitung der mündlichen Prüfung

Du weißt bereits, dass es sich um eine **Partnerprüfung** handelt. Es ist daher sinnvoll, sich zu zweit auf diese Prüfung langfristig vorzubereiten. Am besten ist natürlich ein/-e Mitschüler/-in, mit der oder dem du diese Prüfung vielleicht tatsächlich gemeinsam ablegst. An manchen Schulen sind die Prüfungspaare bekannt. Das folgende Kapitel bietet dir wertvolle **Hinweise zur Vorbereitung** auf die einzelnen Prüfungsteile. Du findest außerdem **Strategien** für eine erfolgreiche Kommunikation, die du auch nach der Prüfung noch gewinnbringend anwenden kannst.

B 2 Berlin: Tipps, Strategien und Übungen zur Vorbereitung

In den folgenden Ausführungen findest du konkrete Tipps und Übungsvorschläge zur gezielten Vorbereitung auf die einzelnen Teile der mündlichen Prüfung. Außerdem werden dir nützliche Redemittel vorgestellt. Da die Prüfung zur mündlichen Sprechfertigkeit eine Partnerprüfung ist, solltest du dir zur Vorbereitung einen Freund oder eine Freundin suchen, mit dem oder der du gemeinsam üben kannst.

B 2.1 Berlin: Prüfungsteil 1 – Kontakt aufnehmen

In diesem Prüfungsteil werden dir und deiner Partnerin / deinem Partner abwechselnd Fragen gestellt, z. B.

– *What's your name?*
– *How old are you?*
– *Where do you live?*
– *Do you have any brothers/sisters/pets/...?*
– *What are your favourite books / sports / free-time activities / ...?*

– *Do you like reading books or magazines / listening to music / ...?*
– *How long have you been living in Berlin?*
– *What are your plans for the weekend / your next holiday / ...?*
– *How did you get to school today?*
– *Please spell your name / surname / the word "...".*

a) Ideen sammeln und strukturieren

Da sich diese Fragen auf bestimmte Themenkomplexe (*topics*) beziehen, lohnt es sich, in der Vorbereitung thematische **Mindmaps** oder **Ideensammlungen** wie die folgende anzufertigen.

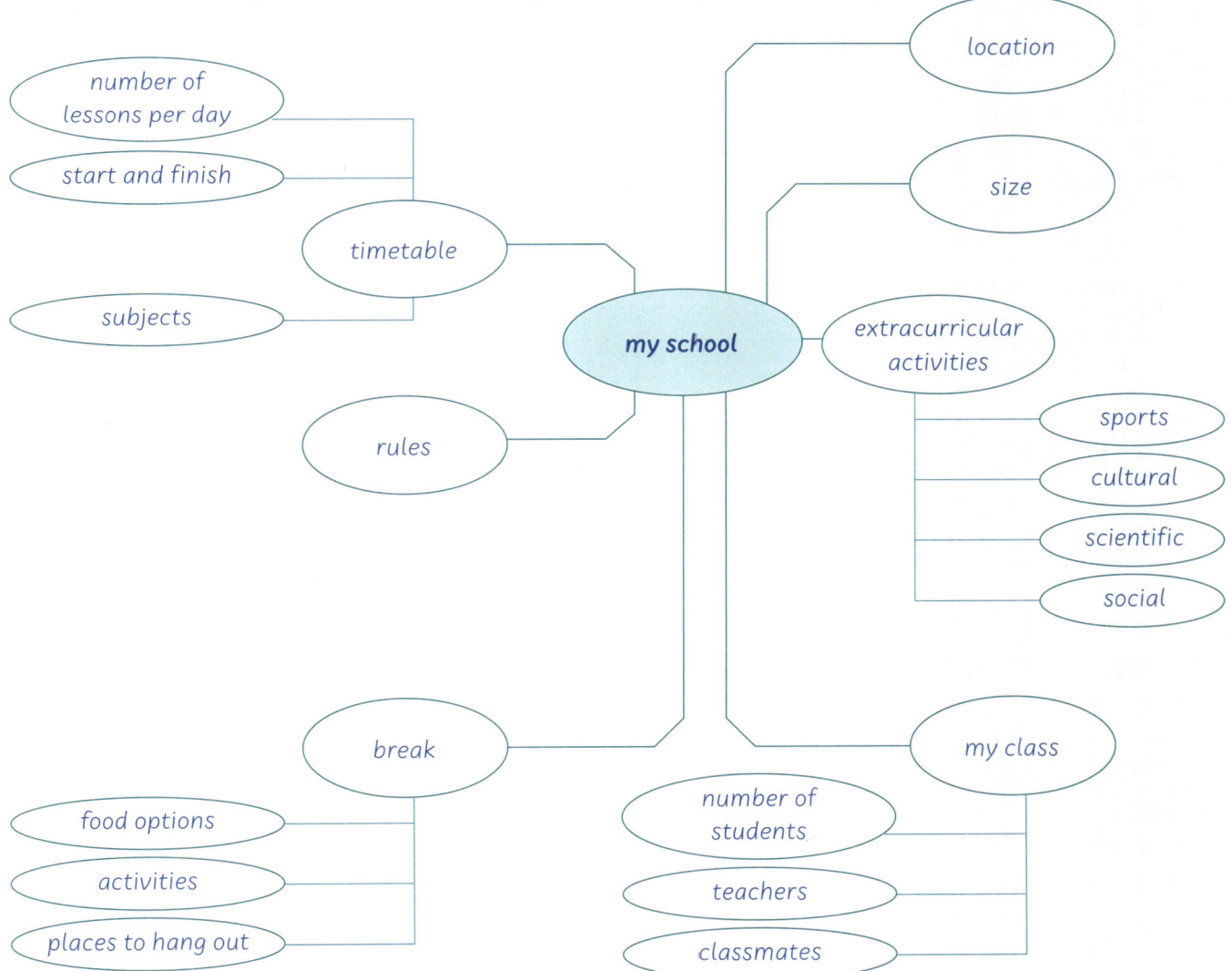

Am besten bereitest du die folgenden Themen auf diese Weise vor:
- *my family and I*
- *hobbies and things I like*
- *where I live*
- *my plans and dreams for the future*
- *my daily routines*
- *my perfect holiday*

b) Redemittel üben

Sieh dir die folgende Tabelle an. In der linken Spalte findest du Fragen, die möglicherweise im ersten Teil der mündlichen Prüfung gestellt werden. Lies die Antwortmöglichkeiten auf der rechten Seite durch und ordne den Fragen jeweils eine passende Antwort zu. Du hast mehr Antworten, als du brauchst.

Questions		Answers	
1	When do you normally get up in the morning?	a	I was at the Baltic Sea with friends.
2	How do you usually get to school? How long does it take you to get to school?	b	Usually I go out with friends on Saturdays and sleep in on Sundays.
3	What do you usually do at weekends?	c	I practised with a partner in class and looked at my lesson notes.
4	What did you do last summer?	d	No, I don't. I think they're all unsafe.
5	What are your plans for next year?	e	Yes, I am. I watch a lot of football and I run every day.
6	What's your favourite subject?	f	Yes, I have a younger sister. Her name is Anne.
7	Are you using any social networking sites?	g	During the week I get up at 6 a. m.
8	How much time a day do you spend in front of the TV?	h	In winter I go by bus and in summer I cycle. I usually need twenty to thirty minutes.
9	Are you interested in sports?	i	I'm hoping to start an apprenticeship as a car mechanic.
10	How did you prepare for this exam?	j	My father works as a cook in a hospital.
		k	I like physics and maths best.
		l	I'm not sure. It depends on what's on. Sometimes an hour a day, sometimes more.

Lösungen für Questions and Answers:

Trage den Buchstaben für die von dir gewählte Antwort ein.

question	1	2	3	4	5	6	7	8	9	10
answer										

Hier kannst du deine persönlichen Antworten zu den Fragen notieren:

1 _____

2 _____

3 _____

4 _____

5 _____

6 _____

7 _____

8 _____

9 _____

10 _____

c) Spielerische Partneraktivitäten zur Vorbereitung

1. **Frage-Antwort-Spiel:** Schreibt diese und ähnliche Fragen auf kleine Karteikärtchen und legt sie auf einen Stapel vor euch. Abwechselnd zieht ihr beide eine Karte und stellt sie der oder dem anderen vor. Fahrt fort, bis der Kartenstapel leer ist.
2. **Memory:** Bereitet zu jeder Frage auch ein Antwortkärtchen vor. Mischt alle Karten und legt sie verdeckt vor euch hin. Abwechselnd deckt ihr nun beide zwei Kärtchen auf. Ergeben diese ein Frage-Antwort-Paar, gehören die Karten euch.
3. **Domino:** Bereitet ein Domino-Spiel mit Fragen und dazu passenden Antworten vor. Spielt anschließend nach den Regeln eines herkömmlichen Dominos.
4. **Stopp die Zeit!:** Abwechselnd erhaltet ihr die Gelegenheit, so viele Sätze und Informationen über euch mitzuteilen wie möglich. Dabei wird die Zeit gestoppt. Gewonnen hat, wer am längsten zusammenhängend über sich sprechen konnte. Dieses Spiel auf Zeit könnt ihr natürlich endlos wiederholen – allein oder zu zweit.

Da ihr in der Prüfung aufgefordert werdet, ein Wort oder mehrere englische Wörter zu buchstabieren, lohnt es sich, die folgenden kleinen Übungsvorschläge in die Vorbereitung mit einzubeziehen.

d) Übungen und Aktivitäten zum Buchstabieren

1. **Wörtergewimmel:** Schreibt ca. 30 englische Wörter auf ein Blatt Papier. Anschließend buchstabiert ihr wahllos einzelne Wörter vorwärts oder rückwärts. Es gilt, möglichst schnell das entsprechende Wort zu finden.
2. Jede/-r von euch sucht sich zehn lange englische Wörter aus dem Wörterbuch aus. Schreibt sie auf ein Blatt Papier. Anschließend buchstabiert ihr sie abwechselnd. Die Partnerin oder der Partner muss das Wort nun im Wörterbuch finden und die Anzahl der Buchstaben notieren. Gewonnen hat, wessen Gesamtbuchstabenzahl am Ende die höhere ist.

B 2.2 Berlin: Prüfungsteil 2 – Etwas aushandeln

Im zweiten Prüfungsteil führst du ein Gespräch mit deiner Partnerin bzw. deinem Partner. Dabei wird von dir erwartet, dass du zu einer vorgegebenen Situation (z. B. einer bevorstehenden Klassenfahrt) Vorschläge unterbreiten und/oder angemessen auf Vorschläge reagieren kannst. Dazu notwendige und nützliche Formulierungen findest du in der folgenden Übersicht.

a) Redemittel zur Diskussion

Making a suggestion (einen Vorschlag machen)	Agreeing with a partner (einem Vorschlag zustimmen)	Disagreeing with a partner (einen Vorschlag ablehnen)
– What do you think of ...? – What about ...?	– That's a great idea. – That sounds good/great. – Yes, OK. – All right, I agree.	– I don't think that's a good idea (because ...) – I'm afraid I can't agree with you. – Well, that's true but ...

b) Zuordnungsübung

Versuche nun, die folgenden ungeordneten Redewendungen und Satzanfänge den passenden Sprechabsichten in der Tabelle zuzuordnen. Ergänze die Übersicht.

How do you feel about ...? | I think so too. | You're absolutely right.

I really think you're wrong because ... | Why don't we ...? | Of course, I agree with you.

I'm sorry, but I don't agree with you. | Personally, I think ...

I can't agree with you. | We could ... | Do you agree?

Let's ... | That's not a great idea because ...

c) Partnerübung zur Vorbereitung

1. Mithilfe der Redewendungen aus a) und b) könnt ihr euer Wissen nun an den folgenden Situationen ausprobieren:

   Task: Discuss the topic(s) and come to a decision – after you have talked about all five options.

You and your friend want to celebrate a joint birthday party. Decide on a format. – costume party – picnic in the park – a night out at the cinema – a night of board and video games – playing laser tag together	Your friends want to go out for an evening together. Where will you go? – cinema – museum – bowling – disco – rock concert
Your class are planning a weekend trip, where will you go? – a farm in Brandenburg – the beach – the mountains – a water park – a friend's garden	You want to lose weight. What can you do to live more healthily? – no fast/junk food – more fruits/vegetables – work out in a gym – walk to school – no coke or other fizzy drinks

TIPP

In der realen Prüfung erhältst du zu der geschilderten Situation anstelle der fünf Optionen kleine Bildimpulse, die dir Ideen geben, um das Gespräch oder die Diskussion zu eröffnen bzw. aufrechtzuhalten. Nutze diese Hilfe, lege die Bilder aber unbedingt beiseite, wenn sie dir unpassend erscheinen oder wenn sie unbekannten Wortschatz verlangen.

TIPP zur Gesprächsführung

Löse dich in diesem Prüfungsteil von der prüfenden Lehrkraft. Wende dich ganz deiner Partnerin bzw. deinem Partner zu und arbeite mit Mimik und Gestik. Nicke ihr oder ihm zu, lächle aufmunternd und nutze das Bildmaterial, um mit dem Finger darauf zu zeigen und das Gespräch authentischer wirken zu lassen.

B 2.3 Berlin: Prüfungsteil 3 – Ein Bild beschreiben

a) Schrittfolge und Redemittel zur Bildbeschreibung

Im dritten Prüfungsteil wird von dir erwartet, dass du zunächst ein aussagekräftiges Bild beschreibst, bevor du im nachfolgenden Prüfungsteil mit deiner Partnerin bzw. deinem Partner Sachverhalte des Bildes diskutierst.

Die nachfolgende Schrittfolge zur Bildbeschreibung wird dir helfen, ruhig und strukturiert vorzugehen.

Schritt 1:	Schau dir das Bild in Ruhe an.
Schritt 2:	Welche Situation wird dargestellt? – Zeigt es eine Straßen- oder Restaurantszene? – Handelt es sich um eine Arbeits- oder Freizeitsituation? Nützliche Redemittel zur Beantwortung der Fragen: – *This picture shows ...* – *This is a picture of ...* – *In this picture I can see ...*

Schritt 3:	Was befindet sich im Mittelpunkt des Bildes?
	– Personen oder zentrale Gegenstände?
	Redemittel:
	– *In the foreground/middle/centre of the picture, there is/are … / I can see …*
	– *She/He is walking along … / sitting inside … / working at …*
	   (ACHTUNG: Handlungen von Personen werden in Bildbeschreibungen mit der Verlaufs-
	   form der Gegenwart – dem *present progressive* – ausgedrückt!)

Schritt 4:	Beschreibe die Person(en): – Was tut/tun sie gerade? – Wer ist/sind die Person/-en? – Welche Emotionen kann man von dem Gesicht / den Gesichtern ablesen? Redemittel: – *She/He is reading … / talking to … / playing with …* – *They're having a meal. / … sunbathing in the sea. / … writing a letter.* – *This person (on the left/right) seems to be a lifeguard.* – *The old man is probably a tourist.* – *You can tell they are enjoying themselves because …* – *The old lady looks very happy … / seems a bit frightened …*
Schritt 5:	Gibt es andere Dinge, die für die Bildaussage wichtig sind? Beschreibe deren Position bzw. Bedeutung. Redemittel: – *In the background there is/are …* – *On the left/right I can see …* – *In the bottom/top left-hand corner … / In the bottom/top right-hand corner …* – *At the top/bottom …* – *There's a … next to … / behind … / in front of … / opposite …* – *It's probably the … because … / It might be … because …*

TIPP

Es kann passieren, dass dir die Vokabel zur Benennung eines zentralen Gegenstandes des Bildes gerade
nicht einfällt. Keine Panik! Versuche einfach, diese Sache zu umschreiben. Erkläre,
– wozu man ihn braucht oder verwendet:
   It's something you need to … / use to …
   It's a kind of tool / bike / container for …
– wie er aussieht (Farbe, Größe, Form):
   It's a red and round vegetable.
– wo man ihn gewöhnlich findet oder aufbewahrt:
   It's something you find in your cupboard / in a forest / near a lake.
– wo er hergestellt wird und/oder aus welchem Material er besteht:
   Wooden sticks that are often used to eat Asian food.

Umschreiben kann man auch durch die Verwendung
– eines **ähnlichen Wortes** (*very big* statt *huge*),
– des **Gegenteils** (*not fast* statt *slow*),
– von Ober- oder Unterbegriffen (*things like knives, forks and spoons* statt *cutlery*) bzw.
– durch die Beschreibung einer **passenden Situation** (*you feel like this when you have to live far away from
   home* statt *homesick*).

b) Übung zum Umschreiben

Schreibe die folgenden deutschen Begriffe auf kleine Zettel. Lege den Zettelstapel dann umgedreht vor dich hin und ziehe nacheinander die Begriffe. Versuche sie auf Englisch zu umschreiben. Die Begriffe, die dir gut bzw. sofort gelingen, lege beiseite. Konzentriere dich nun auf die besonders kniffligen Wörter und überlege, wie du sie mit deinen Worten erklären kannst. Übung macht die Meisterin bzw. den Meister!

Schraubenzieher	Steckdose	Stecknadel	Schubkarre
Flaschenöffner	Stricknadel	Kerzenständer	Backpulver
Fahrradschlauch	Gießkanne	Geldbörse	Mülltonne
Verkehrsampel	Hupe	Antenne	Föhn

Du kannst diese Übung auch zu zweit durchführen. Ihr könnt weitere Begriffe aufschreiben oder aus Umschreibungen den gesuchten Begriff erraten.

c) Übungen zur Bildbeschreibung

Bilder zum Beschreiben findest du in jeder Tageszeitung, Zeitschrift oder im Internet.
Gute Bilder …
– sind farbig,
– zeigen Menschen in ihrem Alltag und
– bieten viele Details zum Beschreiben an.

TIPP

Deine Bildbeschreibung sollte in der Prüfung ungefähr eine Minute dauern. Stell dir eine Eier- oder Stoppuhr, wenn du mit der Beschreibung beginnst. So entwickelst du ein Gefühl für die Zeit.

Partnerübung 1: Wähle ein Bild aus und beschreibe es deinem Gegenüber. Baue einen oder zwei Fehler in deine Beschreibung ein. Kann dein/-e Partner/-in sie finden?

Partnerübung 2: Ihr nehmt beide das gleiche Lehrbuch. Während du ein Bild auswählst und beschreibst, hält dein Gegenüber das Buch geschlossen. Nach Beendigung der Beschreibung erteilst du das Kommando „Ready, steady, go!" und dein/-e Partner/-in versucht so schnell wie möglich das beschriebene Bild zu finden. Ihr könnt euch dabei abwechseln und die „Suchzeit" stoppen.

Partnerübung 3: Wähle ein beliebiges Bild aus und beschreibe es. Währenddessen versucht dein Gegenüber, dieses Bild nach deiner Beschreibung zu zeichnen. Anschließend vergleicht ihr es mit dem Original.

TIPP

Vergiss nicht, …
– in ganzen Sätzen zu sprechen.
– deine Beschreibung zu strukturieren, d. h. mit der dargestellten Situation zu beginnen und danach mit den zentralen Personen/Gegenständen fortzufahren.
– Vermutungen (z. B. über Menschen und deren Gefühle und Stimmungen) anzustellen und zu begründen.
– unwesentliche Details wegzulassen, denn du hast nur etwa eine Minute Zeit.

B 2.4 Berlin: Prüfungsteil 4 – Über ein gegebenes Thema diskutieren

In diesem Prüfungsteil werdet ihr aufgefordert, zu zweit eine Diskussion zu einem vorgegebenen Alltagsthema zu führen. Dieses Thema schließt inhaltlich an die von euch beschriebenen Bilder im Prüfungsteil 3 an. Wenn du also im dritten Prüfungsteil siehst, dass dein Bild oder das deiner Partnerin bzw. deines Partners Menschen bei sportlichen Aktivitäten zeigen, kannst du davon ausgehen, dass ihr im vierten Prüfungsteil die Aufgabe erhalten werdet, ein Gespräch zum Thema Sport und Fitness zu führen.

Folgende Themen (*topics*) könnten dir in diesem Prüfungsteil begegnen:
– *The importance of sports and personal fitness*
– *Free time and weekend activities*
– *What makes the perfect holiday?*
– *Eating habits and a healthy diet*
– *Information technology in your life*
– *City life or country life?*
– *How to save the environment*
– *Summer or winter – what's your season?*
– *Important relationships in your life*
– *Fashion, appearance, style*
– *The impact of media*

Auch hier bietet es sich an, eine **Ideensammlung** zu verschiedenen Themen anzulegen: Was kannst du zu den einzelnen Themen sagen, welche Meinung vertrittst du zu Themen wie „gesunde Ernährung" oder „sinnvolle Freizeitgestaltung"?

TIPP

Lege zu den einzelnen Problemstellungen jeweils eine Karteikarte an, auf der du deine Meinung formulierst und gute Argumente notierst. Du wirst schnell merken, dass sich bestimmte Redewendungen häufig wiederholen. Diese Wiederholungen prägen sich natürlich schnell ein.

Es geht also darum, die eigene Meinung auszudrücken sowie Argumente zu entwickeln und zu begründen. Viele der dazu notwendigen Redemittel findest du bereits im Kapitel B 1.2 a) und b)
Die folgende **Übersicht** zeigt dir noch einmal, wie du deine eigene Meinung ausdrücken kannst.

a) Redemittel zur Meinungsäußerung

> *I think/feel/believe …*   *In my opinion …*   *As I see it …*   *In my view …*

> *It seems to me that …*   *My point of view is that …*

b) Argumentieren
Es reicht natürlich nicht, nur die eigene Meinung zu sagen. Du solltest dich immer bemühen, auch Gründe und Argumente aufzuzählen, die dich zu deiner Überzeugung veranlassen. Da es für viele Problemstellungen zwei Seiten (pro und kontra) gibt, bietet es sich an, eine zweispaltige Tabelle anzulegen, wie z. B. die folgende zum Thema „City or country life? Which do you prefer?".

City life	Country life
– entertainment – short distances – shopping (facilities) – good public transport – ...	– healthy lifestyle – close relationships – close to nature (lakes, ...) – fewer distractions – ...

c) Fragen stellen

Du und deine Partnerin oder dein Partner seid natürlich nicht nur aufgefordert, eure Meinung zum Thema zu vertreten und über euch zu berichten, sondern auch, euch gegenseitig zu befragen. Somit könnt ihr die Richtung des Gesprächs durch eure Fragen aktiv mitbestimmen. Es ist deshalb sinnvoll, sich im Vorfeld auch mögliche Fragen zu den einzelnen Themen zu überlegen und diese zu formulieren. Dabei lassen sich einige Fragestrukturen auf viele Themen übertragen, z. B.

– *What's your favourite ... ?*
– *What do you think about ... ?*
– *Why do/don't you like ... ?*
– *What kind of .... do you have/like/hate ...?*
– *How often do you ... ?*
– *Do you prefer ... or ... ?*
– *Have you ever ... ?*

Wenn ihr diese drei Aspekte a) bis c) auf eurer Ideensammlung schriftlich notiert, könnt ihr sprachlich gut vorbereitet in eine Partnerübungsphase gehen. Hier bietet es sich an, Problemstellungen auf kleine Zettel zu schreiben, diese verdeckt auf den Tisch zu legen und nacheinander umzudrehen. Die daraus entstehenden Diskussionen werden zunächst noch kurz und holprig verlaufen, ihr übt dadurch aber die Gesprächsführung. Am Ende werden die Gespräche zur Routine und vermitteln Spaß an der Diskussion.

Diskussionskärtchen zum Üben

Dies sind Beispiele für Diskussionskärtchen:

City life or country life? What are advantages / disadvantages of either?	Healthy eating → fruit and vegetables only?	Social media – genius or dangerous?	What makes a perfect holiday?
Fast food restaurants should be banned.	Is marriage out of date and a relic from the past?	Veganism is the future for our planet.	Extreme sports – unnecessary risk or great challenge?
Power to the children – voting age should be lowered to 14.	Smartphone bans should be compulsory in all schools for kids under 16.	Appearance is important. Your style is key to success in life.	School's finished and what's next – a gap year, a long holiday or starting work straight away?
What makes the perfect friend? What's most important in a friendship?	AI – will artificial intelligence make all our lives better and easier?	E-sports – real sport or just another word for a gaming addiction?	Gym, gym, gym – is too much fitness bad for you?
Pedestrian cities – all city centres should be car free.	Keeping pets in flats and cities shouldn't be allowed.	Would school uniforms be better for the social atmosphere in schools?	What is part of a healthy lifestyle to you?

Teil B Die mündliche Prüfung

B 1 Brandenburg: Vorbereitung – Let's get ready for the oral test!

B 1.1 Brandenburg: Was wird in der mündlichen Prüfung erwartet?

Bei der Überprüfung der mündlichen Sprechfertigkeit handelt es sich um eine **Gruppenprüfung** von 15–20 Minuten Dauer. Sie erfolgt **ohne Vorbereitungszeit.**

Das Prüfungsgespräch führt dein Englischlehrer bzw. deine Englischlehrerin. Außerdem wird eine zweite Lehrkraft anwesend sein. Diese Lehrkraft beobachtet die Prüfung und fertigt ein Protokoll an. Sie beteiligt sich aber nicht aktiv an der Prüfung.

Das mündliche Prüfungsgespräch besteht aus **drei Teilen.** Überprüft wird deine Fähigkeit, sprachlich korrekt auf verschiedene Gesprächs- oder Bildimpulse zu reagieren, deine Meinung überzeugend auszudrücken und dabei angemessen auf Gesprächspartner/-innen einzugehen.

B 1.2 Brandenburg: Zum Aufbau der mündlichen Prüfung (Gruppenprüfung)

Die mündliche Prüfung setzt sich aus **drei Teilen** zusammen, in denen deine mündliche Sprechfertigkeit auf unterschiedliche Weise überprüft wird:

Teil 1 (ca. 4–6 Minuten): Die prüfende Lehrkraft begrüßt alle Gruppenmitglieder. Sie stellt euch in einem kurzen Gespräch Fragen zur eigenen Person, zu Hobbys und Freizeitaktivitäten, zu Familie und Freunden, aber auch zu Träumen und Hoffnungen. Gegebenenfalls erhaltet ihr auch Gelegenheit, einem der anderen Prüflinge eine Frage zu stellen.

Teil 2 (ca. 5–7 Minuten): Im zweiten Teil der Gruppenprüfung erhaltet ihr nacheinander einen visuellen Impuls (z. B. ein Foto, eine Zeichnung, einen Cartoon mit/ohne Sprechblasen), der euch einen Sprechanlass bieten wird. Alle Bilder beziehen sich auf ein gemeinsames Thema, zu dem sich jeder Prüfling zusammenhängend äußern soll.

Teil 3 (ca. 6–7 Minuten): Ausgehend vom Thema der Sprechimpulse im Teil 2 der Prüfung erhaltet ihr nun von der prüfenden Lehrkraft eine Aufgaben- bzw. Problemstellung. Sie dient euch zum gemeinsamen Gedankenaustausch, aber auch zur Diskussion. In Form eines kleinen Rollenspiels sollt ihr hier Argumente entwickeln und Problemlösungen herbeiführen.

> **INFO** zum Prüfungsablauf
>
> Die Überprüfung der mündlichen Sprechfertigkeit erfolgt in drei Teilen:
> 1. **Dialogisches Sprechen/Interview:** Small Talk
> 2. **Ein Bild (Foto, Cartoon) beschreiben:** zusammenhängend sprechen
> 3. **Über ein Thema diskutieren:** Gruppengespräch

Prüfungsteil	Mögliche Themen und Inhalte	Übungshinweise
PT 1: Dialogisches Sprechen / Interview	– Fragen beantworten zu Person, Familie, Freunden, Freizeit und Hobbys, Wünschen und Hoffnungen	Tipps und Übungen zu diesem Prüfungsteil findest du auf S. 104–106
PT 2: Zusammenhängendes monologisches Sprechen	– Gesunde Lebensweise, Formen des Zusammenlebens, soziales Engagement, sinnvolle Freizeitgestaltung, Essgewohnheiten, Freundschaft und Liebe usw.	Tipps und Übungen zur Bildbeschreibung findest du auf S. 106
PT 3: Dialogisches Sprechen / Interaktion		Tipps und Übungen zu diesem Prüfungsteil findest du auf S. 108–109

B 1.3 Brandenburg: Kriterien der Bewertung

Die prüfende Lehrkraft und die/der Protokollierende nehmen unmittelbar nach der Prüfung die Bewertung deiner Sprechleistung vor. Dabei stehen vier Bewertungskriterien im Mittelpunkt, die gleichwertig in die Endbeurteilung deiner Leistung einfließen:

– die kommunikative Kompetenz,

– der Gesprächsbeitrag,

– Grammatik und Wortschatz, und

– die Aussprache.

Kommunikative Kompetenz	Gesprächsbeitrag	Grammatik und Wortschatz	Aussprache
– Gelingt es dir, Gespräche zu eröffnen, fortzuführen und zu beenden?	– Kannst du deine Gedanken sinnvoll strukturieren und ausdrücken?	– Gelingt es dir, grammatische Strukturen möglichst fehlerfrei zu verwenden (z. B. bei der Fragebildung und den Zeitformen)?	– Sind deine Aussprache und Intonation so gut, dass man dich problemlos versteht?
– Sprichst du verständlich und in vollständigen Sätzen?	– Sprichst du zum Thema?	– Verfügst du über einen Wortschatz, der es dir ermöglicht, viele Themen spontan und verständlich zu diskutieren?	– Sprichst du flüssig?
– Stellst du verständliche Fragen und gehst auf die Äußerungen deines Gegenübers ein?	– Gehst du auf deine Gesprächspartner/-innen ein?		

B 1.4 Brandenburg: Tipps zur Vorbereitung der mündlichen Prüfung

Du weißt bereits, dass es sich um eine Gruppenprüfung handelt. Es ist daher sinnvoll, sich gemeinsam auf diese Prüfung langfristig vorzubereiten. Am besten sind natürlich Mitschüler/-innen, mit denen du vielleicht die Prüfung gemeinsam ablegen wirst. An manchen Schulen sind die Prüfungsgruppen bekannt.

Das folgende Kapitel bietet dir wertvolle **Hinweise zur Vorbereitung** auf die einzelnen Prüfungsteile. Du findest außerdem **Strategien** für eine erfolgreiche Kommunikation, die du auch nach der Prüfung noch gewinnbringend anwenden kannst.

B 2 Brandenburg: Tipps, Strategien und Übungen zur Vorbereitung

In den folgenden Ausführungen findest du konkrete Tipps und Übungsvorschläge zur gezielten Vorbereitung auf die einzelnen Teile der mündlichen Prüfung. Außerdem werden dir nützliche Redemittel vorgestellt. Da die Prüfung zur mündlichen Sprechfertigkeit eine Gruppenprüfung ist, solltest du dir zur Vorbereitung Freundinnen und Freunde suchen, mit denen du gemeinsam üben kannst.

B 2.1 Brandenburg: Prüfungsteil 1 – Kontakt aufnehmen

In diesem Prüfungsteil werden dir und deinen Gruppenmitgliedern abwechselnd Fragen gestellt, z. B.

- *What's your name?*
- *How old are you?*
- *Where do you live?*
- *Do you have any brothers/sisters/pets/...?*
- *What are your favourite books / sports / free-time activities / subjects at school / ...?*
- *Do you like reading books or magazines / listening to music / ...?*
- *How long have you been living in Berlin?*
- *What are your plans for the weekend / your next holiday / ...?*
- *How did you get to school today?*

a) Ideen sammeln und strukturieren

Da sich diese Fragen auf bestimmte Themenkomplexe (*topics*) beziehen, lohnt es sich in Vorbereitung thematische **Mindmaps** oder **Ideensammlungen** anzufertigen, z. B. zu diesen Themen:

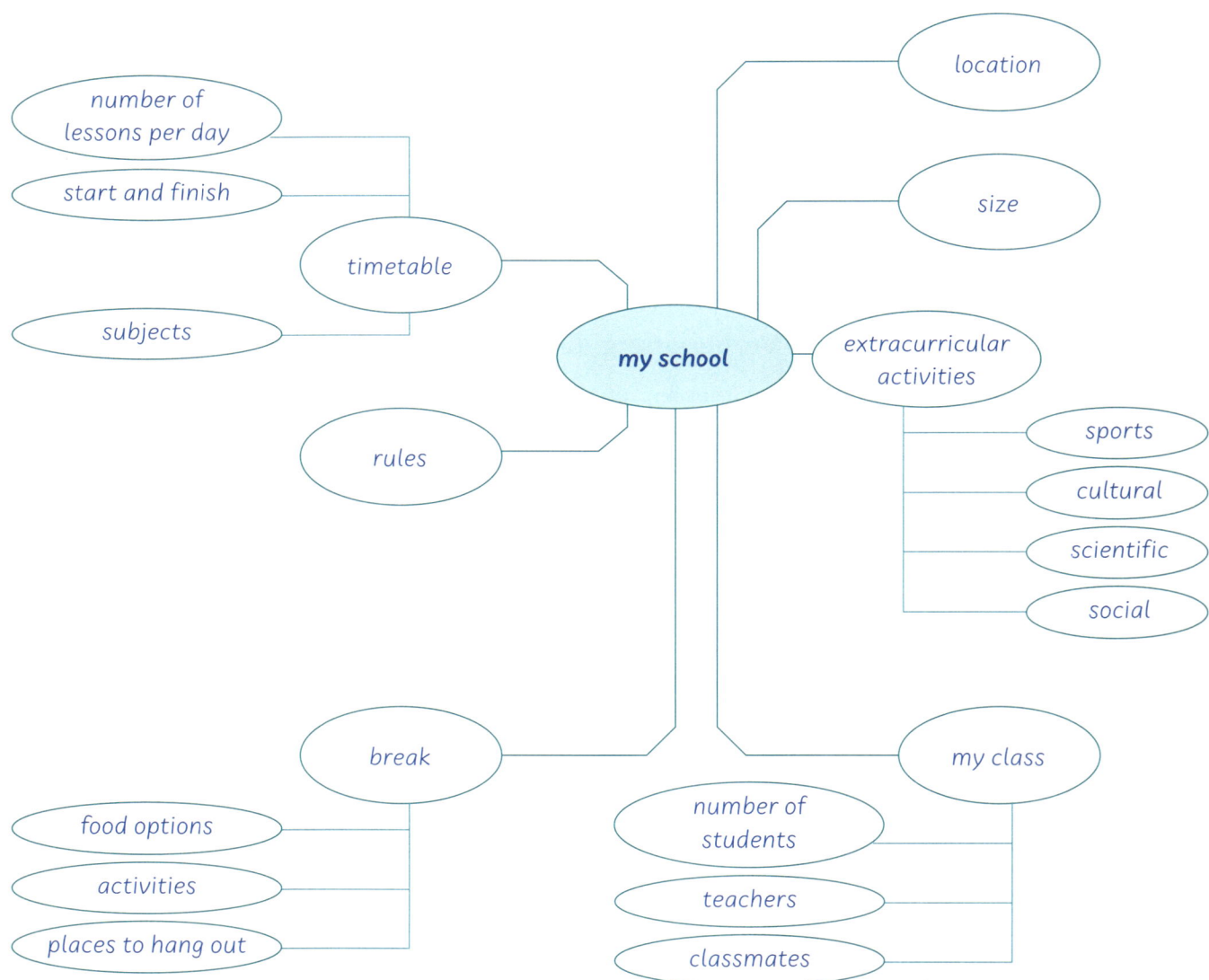

Am besten bereitest du die folgenden Themen auf diese Weise vor:
– *my family and I*
– *hobbies and things I like*
– *where I live*
– *my plans and dreams for the future*
– *my daily routines*
– *my perfect holiday*

TIPP zur Vorbereitung

Das Anlegen dieser Themenlisten bzw. Mindmaps, das damit verbundene Nachdenken über mögliche Inhalte und das Nachschlagen von persönlich bedeutsamen Vokabeln sind eine ideale Vorbereitung auf den ersten Prüfungsteil. Es gibt dir etwas „zum Anfassen" und damit Struktur und Sicherheit.

b) Redemittel üben

Sieh dir die folgende Tabelle an. In der linken Spalte findest du Fragen, die möglicherweise im ersten Teil der mündlichen Prüfung gestellt werden. Lies die Antwortmöglichkeiten auf der rechten Seite durch und ordne den Fragen jeweils eine passende Antwort zu. Du hast mehr Antworten, als du brauchst.

	Questions		Answers
1	When do you normally get up in the morning?	a	I was at the Baltic Sea with friends.
2	How do you usually get to school? How long does it take you to get to school?	b	Usually I go out with friends on Saturdays and sleep in on Sundays.
3	What do you usually do at weekends?	c	I practised with a partner in class and looked at my lesson notes.
4	What did you do last summer?	d	No, I don't. I think they're all unsafe.
5	What are your plans for next year?	e	Yes, I am. I watch a lot of football and I run every day.
6	What's your favourite subject?	f	Yes, I have a younger sister. Her name is Anne.
7	Are you using any social networking sites?	g	During the week I get up at 6 a.m.
8	How much time a day do you spend in front of the TV?	h	In winter I go by bus and in summer I cycle. I usually need twenty to thirty minutes.
9	Are you interested in sports?	i	I'm hoping to start an apprenticeship as a car mechanic.
10	How did you prepare for this exam?	j	My father works as a cook in a hospital.
		k	I like physics and maths best.
		l	I'm not sure. It depends on what's on. Sometimes an hour a day, sometimes more.

Lösungen für Questions and Answers:

Trage den Buchstaben für die von dir gewählte Antwort ein.

question	1	2	3	4	5	6	7	8	9	10
answer										

Hier kannst du deine persönlichen Antworten zu den Fragen notieren:

1 _____

2 _____

3 _____

4 _____

5 _____

6 _____

7 _____

8 _____

9 _____

10 _____

c) Spielerische Aktivitäten zur Vorbereitung

1. **Frage-Antwort-Spiel:** Schreibt diese und ähnliche Fragen auf kleine Karteikärtchen und legt sie auf einen Stapel vor euch. Abwechselnd zieht jeder von euch eine Karte und stellt sie den anderen vor. Fahrt fort, bis der Kartenstapel leer ist.
2. **Memory:** Bereitet zu jeder Frage auch ein Antwortkärtchen vor. Mischt alle Karten und legt sie verdeckt vor euch hin. Abwechselnd deckt nun jeder zwei Kärtchen auf. Ergeben diese ein Frage-Antwort-Paar, gehören die Karten euch.
3. **Domino:** Bereitet ein Domino-Spiel mit Fragen und dazu passenden Antworten vor. Spielt anschließend nach den Regeln eines herkömmlichen Dominos.
4. **Stopp die Zeit!:** Abwechselnd erhaltet ihr die Gelegenheit, so viele Sätze und Informationen über euch mitzuteilen wie möglich. Dabei wird die Zeit gestoppt. Gewonnen hat, wer am längsten zusammenhängend über sich sprechen konnte. Dieses Spiel auf Zeit könnt ihr natürlich endlos wiederholen – allein oder in der Gruppe.

B 2.2 Brandenburg: Prüfungsteil 2 – Bildbeschreibung / Monologisches Sprechen

Im zweiten Prüfungsteil erhaltet ihr nacheinander einen visuellen Impuls (z. B. eine Zeichnung, ein Foto oder einen Cartoon) zu einem gemeinsamen Thema. Hier wird von dir erwartet, dass du zunächst das Bild beschreibst und dich zu der dargestellten Thematik möglichst ausführlich äußerst.

a) Schrittfolge und Redemittel

Die nachfolgende Schrittfolge wird dir helfen, in diesem Prüfungsteil ruhig und strukturiert vorzugehen.

Schritt 1:	Schau dir das Bild in Ruhe an.
Schritt 2:	Welche Situation wird dargestellt? – Zeigt es eine Straßen- oder Restaurantszene? – Handelt es sich um eine Arbeits- oder Freizeitsituation? Nützliche Redemittel zur Beantwortung der Fragen: – *This picture shows …* – *This is a picture of …* – *In this picture I can see …*

Schritt 3:	Was befindet sich im Mittelpunkt des Bildes? – Personen oder zentrale Gegenstände? Redemittel: – *In the foreground/middle/centre of the picture there is/are … / I can see …* – *She/He is walking along … / sitting inside … / working at …* (ACHTUNG: Handlungen von Personen werden in Bildbeschreibungen mit der Verlaufsform der Gegenwart – dem *present progressive* – ausgedrückt!)
Schritt 4:	Beschreibe die Person(en): – Was tut/tun sie gerade? – Wer ist/sind die Person/-en? – Welche Emotionen kann man von dem Gesicht / den Gesichtern ablesen? Redemittel: – *She/He is reading … / talking to … / playing with …* – *They're having a meal. / … sunbathing in the sea. / … writing a letter.* – *This person (on the left/right) seems to be a lifeguard.* – *The old man is probably a tourist.* – *You can tell they are enjoying themselves because …* – *The old lady looks very happy … / seems a bit frightened …*
Schritt 5:	Gibt es andere Dinge, die für die Bildaussage wichtig sind? Beschreibe deren Position bzw. Bedeutung. Redemittel: – *In the background there is/are …* – *On the left/right I can see …* – *In the bottom/top left-hand corner … / In the bottom/top right-hand corner …* – *At the top/bottom …* – *There's a … next to … / behind … / in front of … / opposite …* – *It's probably the … because … / It might be … because …*
Schritt 6:	Woran erinnert dich dieses Bild? Was hat es mit dir bzw. deinem Leben zu tun? Welche Bedeutung hat die Thematik für dich? – *The picture/cartoon makes me think of … / reminds me of …* – *Like/Unlike the person in the picture/cartoon, I …* – *If I were/saw … I would …. because …* – *I personally think (that) … because …* – *I (dis)agree with the message because …* – *It's true that …*

b) Übung zum Umschreiben

Schreibe die folgenden deutschen Begriffe auf kleine Zettel. Lege den Zettelstapel dann umgedreht vor dich hin und ziehe nacheinander die Begriffe. Versuche sie auf Englisch zu umschreiben. Die Begriffe, die dir gut bzw. sofort gelingen, lege beiseite. Konzentriere dich nun auf die besonders kniffligen Wörter und überlege, wie du sie mit deinen Worten erklären kannst. Übung macht die Meisterin bzw. den Meister!

Schraubenzieher	Steckdose	Stecknadel	Schubkarre
Flaschenöffner	Stricknadel	Kerzenständer	Backpulver
Fahrradschlauch	Gießkanne	Geldbörse	Mülltonne
Verkehrsampel	Hupe	Antenne	Föhn

Du kannst diese Übung auch zu zweit durchführen. Ihr könnt weitere Begriffe aufschreiben oder aus Umschreibungen den gesuchten Begriff erraten.

c) Übungen zur Beschreibung von Bildern oder Cartoons

Bilder (Fotos, Zeichnungen oder Cartoons) zum Beschreiben findest du in jeder Tageszeitung, Zeitschrift oder im Internet.

Gute Bilder …
– sind farbig,
– zeigen Menschen in ihrem Alltag und
– bieten viele Details zum Beschreiben an.

TIPP

Vergiss nicht, …
– in ganzen Sätzen zu sprechen.
– deine Beschreibung zu strukturieren, d. h. mit der dargestellten Situation zu beginnen und danach mit den zentralen Personen/Gegenständen fortzufahren.
– Vermutungen (z. B. über Menschen und deren Gefühle und Stimmungen) anzustellen und zu begründen.
– unwesentliche Details wegzulassen, denn du hast nur etwa eine Minute Zeit.

B 2.3 Brandenburg: Prüfungsteil 3 – Über ein gegebenes Thema diskutieren

In diesem Prüfungsteil wirst du aufgefordert, eine Diskussion zu einem vorgegebenen Alltagsthema zu führen. Dieses Thema schließt inhaltlich an die von euch beschriebenen Bilder im Prüfungsteil 3 an. Wenn du also im zweiten Prüfungsteil siehst, dass eure Bilder z. B. Menschen bei sportlichen Aktivitäten zeigen, kannst du davon ausgehen, dass ihr im dritten Prüfungsteil die Aufgabe erhalten werdet, ein Gespräch zum Thema Sport und Fitness zu führen.

Folgende Themen (*topics*) könnten dir in diesem Prüfungsteil begegnen:
– *The importance of sports and personal fitness*
– *Free time and weekend activities*
– *What makes the perfect holiday?*
– *Eating habits and a healthy diet*
– *Information technology in your life*
– *City life or country life?*
– *How to save the environment*
– *Summer or winter – what's your season?*
– *Important relationships in your life*
– *Fashion, appearance, style*
– *The impact of media*

Auch hier bietet es sich an, eine **Ideensammlung** zu verschiedenen Themen anzulegen: Was kannst du zu den einzelnen Themen sagen, welche Meinung vertrittst du zu Themen wie „gesunde Ernährung" oder „sinnvolle Freizeitgestaltung"?

TIPP

Lege zu den einzelnen Problemstellungen jeweils eine Karteikarte an, auf der du deine Meinung formulierst und gute Argumente notierst. Du wirst schnell merken, dass sich bestimmte Redewendungen häufig wiederholen. Diese Wiederholungen prägen sich natürlich schnell ein.

Es geht also darum, die eigene Meinung auszudrücken sowie Argumente zu entwickeln und zu begründen. Viele der dazu notwendigen Redemittel findest du bereits im Kapitel B 1.2 a) und b)
Die folgende **Übersicht** zeigt dir noch einmal, wie du deine eigene Meinung ausdrücken kannst.

a) Redemittel zur Meinungsäußerung

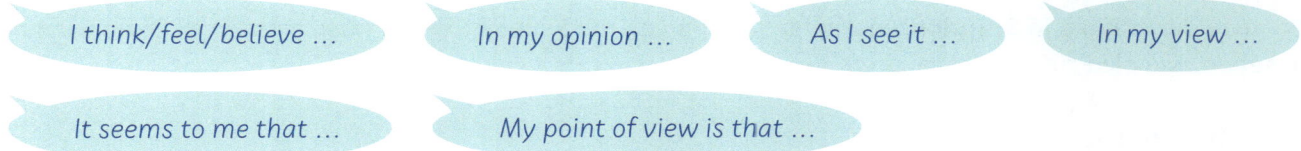

I think/feel/believe …   *In my opinion …*   *As I see it …*   *In my view …*

It seems to me that …   *My point of view is that …*

b) Argumentieren

Es reicht natürlich nicht, nur die eigene Meinung zu sagen. Du solltest dich immer bemühen, auch Gründe und Argumente aufzuzählen, die dich zu deiner Überzeugung veranlassen. Da es für viele Problemstellungen zwei Seiten (pro und kontra) gibt, bietet es sich an, eine zweispaltige Tabelle anzulegen, wie z. B. die folgende zum Thema „City or country life? Which do you prefer?".

City life	Country life
– entertainment – short distances – shopping (facilities) – good public transport – …	– healthy lifestyle – close relationships – close to nature (lakes, …) – fewer distractions – …

c) Fragen stellen

Ihr seid natürlich nicht nur aufgefordert, eure Meinung zum Thema zu vertreten und über euch zu berichten, sondern auch, euch gegenseitig zu befragen. Somit könnt ihr die Richtung des Gesprächs durch eure Fragen aktiv mitbestimmen. Es ist deshalb sinnvoll, sich im Vorfeld auch mögliche Fragen zu den einzelnen Themen zu überlegen und diese zu formulieren. Dabei lassen sich einige Fragestrukturen auf viele Themen übertragen, z. B.

– *What's your favourite … ?*
– *What do you think about … ?*
– *Why do/don't you like … ?*
– *What kind of …. do you have/like/hate/…?*
– *How often do you … ?*
– *Do you prefer … or … ?*
– *Have you ever … ?*

Wenn ihr diese drei Aspekte a) bis c) auf eurer Ideensammlung schriftlich notiert, könnt ihr sprachlich gut vorbereitet in eine Partnerübungsphase gehen. Hier bietet es sich an, Problemstellungen auf kleine Zettel zu schreiben, diese verdeckt auf den Tisch zu legen und nacheinander umzudrehen. Die daraus entstehenden Diskussionen werden zunächst noch kurz und holprig verlaufen, ihr übt dadurch aber die Gesprächsführung. Am Ende werden die Gespräche zur Routine und vermitteln Spaß an der Diskussion.

B 3 Speaking Test / Oral Exam:

Beispiele zur Überprüfung der mündlichen Sprechfertigkeit

In diesem Teil findest du drei vollständige Prüfungsbeispiele, die dem Muster der mündlichen Prüfung in **Berlin** folgen. Sie verdeutlichen dir noch einmal den Ablauf der mündlichen Prüfung und geben euch die Möglichkeit, die Prüfungssituation nachzugestalten und durch wiederholte Übung mehr Sicherheit zu gewinnen. Wenn du die Prüfung in **Brandenburg** ablegst, schau dir die Seiten 102–109 noch einmal an. Dann kannst du sehen, wie die Prüfung dort abläuft.

B 3.1 Speaking Test 1

Part 1: Warming Up
Your teacher might say:

> Good morning. Please come in and take a seat for your oral exam.
> I'm going to ask you some questions and give you some tasks. Ms/Mr X is here
> to listen to us and take notes.

	CANDIDATE A	CANDIDATE B
Answer your teacher's questions.	What's your name/surname? … Can you spell that for me, please?	
		And what about you? … Can you spell your name too, please?
		How did you get to school today?
	And what about you? (How did you get here?)	
	What do you usually do at weekends?	And what about you?
		Are you interested in sports? Which?
	And what's your favourite sport?	
	How often do you train/watch/do this sport?	
		And you? How often do you do sports?
		What are your plans for this summer?
	And what about you? What are your plans for the summer?	
	Thank you very much. That's the end of part one.	

Part 2: Agreeing and Disagreeing

Your teacher:

I'm going to describe a situation to you: Your friend has moved into a new home. Now he/she has invited you to a flat-warming party. You would like to take him/her a present. Look at the ideas in the picture below and discuss them with your partner. Together you must decide on the best present for your friend.

Part 3: Describing a Picture

Your teacher:

Now I'm going to give each of you a picture.

Picture for Candidate A:

Candidate A –
this is your picture.
Please show it to
your partner
(Candidate B) and
talk about it (alone).

Candidate B – you
just listen to your
partner.

Picture for Candidate B:

Here is your picture,
Candidate B.
Please, look at
it, show it to your
partner (Candidate
A) and talk about it
(alone).

Candidate A – you
just listen to your
partner now.

Part 4: Discussing a Topic

Your teacher:

You both had photographs which showed people using a computer or a mobile phone. Now I'd like you to talk together about electronic media/gadgets today. How important are they to you? How often do you use computers, mobile phones or other gadgets? What for? What are the advantages or, maybe, dangers of modern electronic media?

B 3.2 Speaking Test 2

Part 1: Warming Up
Your teacher might say:

*Good morning. Please come in and
take a seat for your oral exam.
I'm going to ask you some questions and
give you some tasks. Ms/Mr X is here
to listen to us and take notes.*

	CANDIDATE A	CANDIDATE B
Answer your teacher's questions.	Where do you live?	
		And you? Where do you live?
		When do you usually get up in the morning?
	And what about you? When do you normally get up?	
		Do you have any brothers or sisters? What are their names? Can you spell your sister's/brother's name?
	Do you have any brothers or sisters? What are their names? Can you spell that, please?	
	What did you do last night?	
		And you? (What did you do?)
		Do you have a favourite TV programme? Which?
	And what about you?	
		What are your plans for next year?
	And what are yours?	
	Thank you very much. That's the end of part one.	

Part 2: Agreeing and Disagreeing

Your teacher:

I'm going to describe a situation to you: The end of tenth grade is coming up. Your form teacher has suggested a final day out for your class as a treat. Look at the ideas below and discuss what kind of activity would be the best idea for your class.

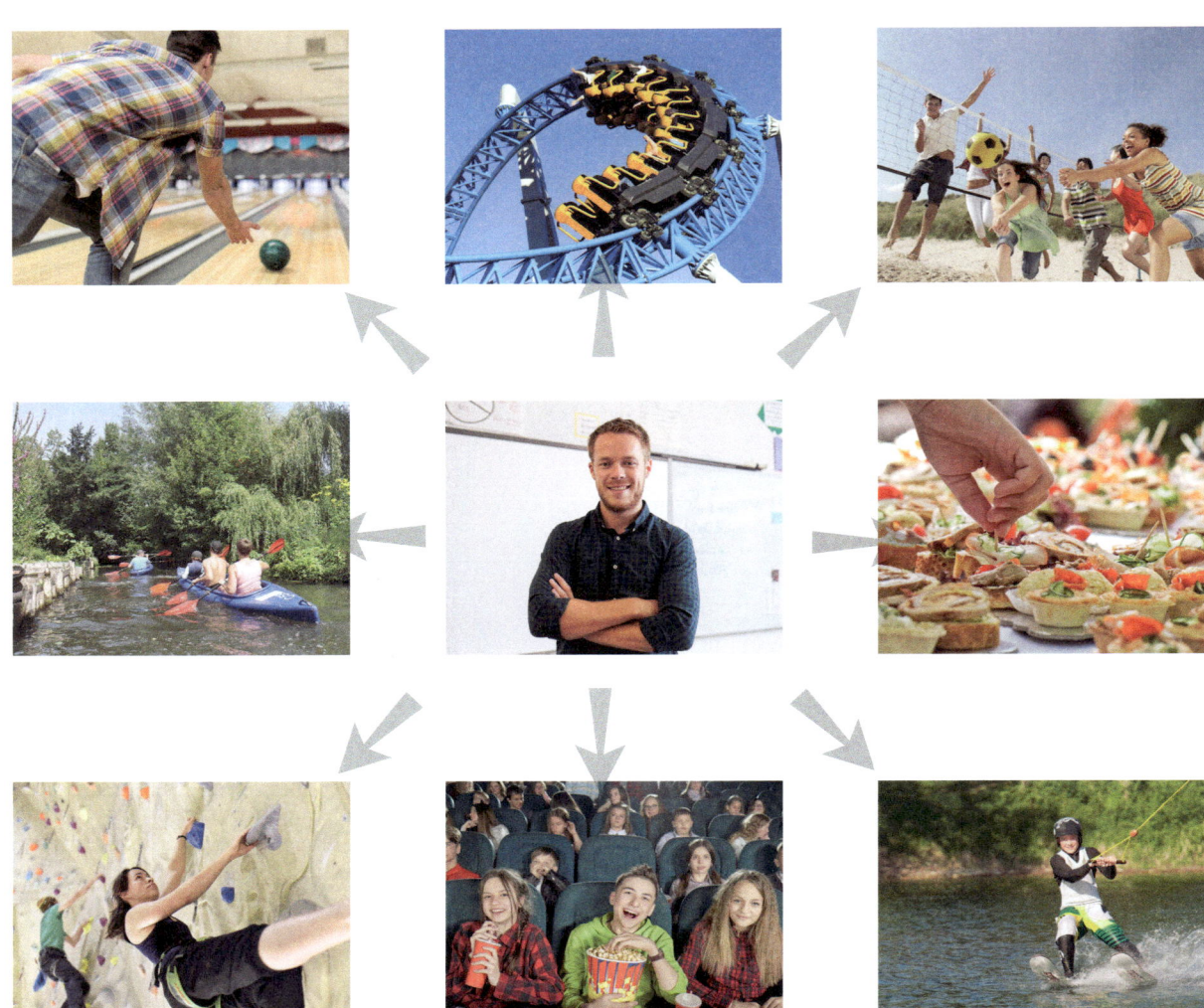

Part 3: Describing a Picture

Your teacher:

Now I'm going to give each of you a picture.

Picture for Candidate A:

Candidate A –
this is your picture.
Please show it to
your partner
(Candidate B) and
talk about it (alone).

Candidate B – you
just listen to your
partner.

Picture for Candidate B:

Here is your picture,
Candidate B.
Please, look at
it, show it to your
partner (Candidate
A) and talk about it
(alone).

Candidate A – you
just listen to your
partner now.

Part 4: Discussing a Topic

Your teacher:

You both had photographs which showed people spending their free time in different ways. Now I'd like you to talk together about your free-time activities. What do you like or hate doing? Who do you spend your free time with? What about weekends? How important is going out to you? Is money an important factor in your free time?

B 3.3 Speaking Test 3

Part 1: Warming Up

Your teacher might say:

Good morning. Please come in and take a seat for your oral exam. I'm going to ask you some questions and give you some tasks. Ms/Mr X is here to listen to us and take notes.

	CANDIDATE A	CANDIDATE B
Answer your teacher's questions.	What's your surname? Can you spell that, please?	
		And you? What's your surname? How do you spell that?
		How did you get to school today?
	And what about you? How did you get to school today?	
		What do you do in your free time?
	And you? What do you do in your free time?	
	What did you do last weekend?	
		And you? (What did you do?)
		Do you have a pet? What kind?
	And what about you?	
		What are your favourite subjects at school?
	And what are yours?	
	Thank you very much. That's the end of part one.	

Part 2: Agreeing and Disagreeing

Your teacher:

I'm going to describe a situation to you: You want to spend a weekend camping with a friend and you can't take a lot of luggage. Look at the ideas below and dicuss them with a partner. Decide on a maximum of six things to take.

Part 3: Describing a Picture

Your teacher:

Now I'm going to give each of you a picture.

Picture for Candidate A:

Candidate A –
this is your picture.
Please show it to
your partner
(Candidate B) and
talk about it (alone).

Candidate B – you
just listen to your
partner.

Picture for Candidate B:

Here is your picture,
Candidate B.
Please, look at
it, show it to your
partner (Candidate
A) and talk about it
(alone).

Candidate A – you
just listen to your
partner now.

Part 4: Discussing a Topic

Your teacher:

You both had photographs which showed people having their meals in different ways. Now I'd like you to talk together about your eating habits. What is your favourite food or meal? What makes a healthy meal? What about fast food? How important is eating out to you? How can teenagers improve their eating habits?

B 4 Redemittel und Wendungen zur Gesprächsführung:
A survival bag of phrases for your oral exam

1) Expressing an opinion

"I think that ..."

I think/feel/believe ...
In my opinion ...
As I see it ...
In my view ...
It seems to me that ...
My point of view is that ...
I'm sure/convinced that ...

2) Asking for an opinion

"I want to find out what my partner thinks."

What do you think about ... (this)?
What's your opinion about ... (this)?
How do you feel about ... (this)?
What do you think?
Do you have any ideas?
What about you?

3) If you didn't understand your partner

"I don't understand what my partner said/means."

Sorry, I didn't quite understand/get that.
Pardon?
Could you say that again, please?
Could you repeat that, please?
What exactly do you mean?
Do you mean ...?
Could you explain that again, please?
Sorry, what was your question?

4) Making suggestions

"I have an idea."

What about ...?
Let's ...
I think ... would be a great idea because ...
Shouldn't we ...?
In my opinion we should ...
Why don't we ...?
I'd suggest we should ...
The best thing would be to ...

5) Agreeing

"My partner is right."

Great idea.
Brilliant. Let's do that.
I (absolutely) agree with you.
You're right.
Of course. I think so too.

6) Disagreeing

"I think my partner is wrong."

Good idea, but ...
Maybe, but I'd prefer ...
I think ... would be better.
I'm not sure this is such a good idea.
I can see your point, but I think ...
No, I can't agree with you.
Sorry, but I have to disagree with you.
I think you're wrong because ...

7) Showing interest in what your partner is saying

"That's interesting."

Really?
I didn't know that.
I see ...
That's interesting/fascinating/amazing.
That sounds good/interesting.

8) How to buy yourself time (to think) in a conversation

"I need more time to think of an answer."

That's a good/difficult question ...
I've never thought about this before ...
I'm not sure ...
Let me think for a second ...
It depends on ... / Well, ...

Quellenverzeichnis

Textquellen

57 Jane Jordan: „Jobben auf dem Reiterhof": *INITIATIVE auslandszeit*, Rheda-Wiedenbrück, EJ nicht angegeben; https://www.farmarbeit. de/pferdejob-groemitz.html (verändert; Zugriff: 20.02.2024)

88 Leo Hickman: „Britain's problem with pets: they're bad for the planet"; *The Guardian*, London, 13.11.2009; https://www.theguardian. com/environment/2009/nov/13/ethical-living-carbon-emissions (verändert; Zugriff: 20.02.2024)

Hörquellen

78 Ad 3: „Metropolitan Police, 'necklace'", *Haymarket Media Group Ltd.*, London, EJ nicht angegeben, https://www.campaignlive.co.uk/ article/top-10-radio-ads-2012/1163736 (verändert, Zugriff: 20.02.2024); Ad 4: Jennifer Harmon, „Commercial For Nicer Living: The Gift Of Doing Nothing", *NPR*, Washington, D.C., 03.02.2017, https://www.npr.org/2017/02/03/513311295/commercial-for-nicer-living-the-gift-of-doing-nothing (verändert, 20.02.2024)

Bildquellen

|Alamy Stock Photo (RMB), Abingdon/Oxfordshire: Arco Images GmbH/Lacz, G. 60.3; Cultura RM 60.4; De Rueda Roige, Jordi 41.1; du Feu, Geoff 27.5; Dwyer, Michael 67.7; Gasson, Adam 115.2; Holmes, Robert 84.2; imagebroker 84.3; Jeff Gilbert 67.2; Oleksiy Maksymenko 54.1; parkerphotography 76.2. |dreamstime.com, Brentwood: Martinmark 67.3. |Feldhaus, Hans-Jürgen, Münster: 5.4, 19.1, 19.2, 19.3, 19.4, 19.5, 19.6, 19.7, 19.8, 19.9, 20.1, 20.2, 20.3, 20.4, 20.5, 20.6, 20.7, 20.8, 21.1, 22.1, 23.1, 39.1, 42.1, 43.1, 44.1, 59.1, 61.1, 62.1, 63.1, 75.1, 78.1, 79.1, 80.1. |fotolia.com, New York: A_Lein 76.5; arsdigital 83.5; arthurdent 111.8; autofocus67 60.2; benjaminnolte 39.4; Bernd_Leitner 59.6; Brian Jackson 74.2; CandyBox Images 49.5; contrastwerkstatt 49.7; corepics 77.4; Dan Race 10.7; dispicture 40.1; froxx 40.2; Haase, Nadine 60.1; hansenn 12.3; JackF 49.6, 112.2; Jens Ottoson 117.6; ksena32 86.1; marcus_hofmann 111.4; micromonkey 36.1; Monkey Business 118.2; nakedking 60.5; PhotoSG 40.3; Race, Dan 39.2; Sanders, Gina 39.3; Syda Productions 114.1; VRD 117.8; wildworx 115.1. |iStockphoto.com, Calgary: AaronAmat 48.1; amriphoto 57.1; anandoart 67.6; BilevichOlga 76.7; bob_bosewell 48.2; claudiodivizia 2.1; clubfoto 60.7; Damir Khabirov 27.1; David Coleman Photography 43.2; Deagreez 27.2; DisobeyArt 76.4; FatCamera 67.4; Jane_Kelly Titel, 1.2; lisafx 10.4; mashabuba 72.1; MaxFX 111.1; MorganLeFaye 111.5; Motortion 77.8; nilimage 66.1; nndanko 71.1; Photodjo 77.2; Poike 66.2; Ridofranz 27.3; Roman Tiraspolsky 118.1; shironosov 48.5; SolStock 84.1; spooh 83.1; stockfour 27.4; tomazl 67.1; VisualField 111.3. |Shutterstock.com, New York: 1000 Words 41.2; Albert Pego 83.3; Black, Ruth 60.8; Chernyshev, Kirill 76.1; Gorodenkoff 77.3; izikMD 117.1; JeniFoto 76.6; LiliGraphie 55.1; Lorenza Ochoa 79.2; Molchanov, Dmitry 59.7; Monkey Business I 114.5; Peter_Fleming 76.8; spaxiax 117.5; supparsorn 117.3; Suriya KK 12.4; theshots.co 34.1; Zai Di 79.4; Zhuravlev Andrey 79.3. |stock.adobe.com, Dublin: 9nong 82.1; alexlmx 74.1; alice_photo 87.1; Andrey ZH 114.2; AR 111.7; artbox_of_life 117.7; Atkins, Peter 59.2; bolderdi15 10.5; contrastwerkstatt 59.8, 66.5; Cookie Studio Titel, 1.1; Countrypixel 57.2; Cristian 10.6; DDRockstar 82.2; Dietl, Jeanette 48.3; dizelen 49.4; Ernst, Daniel 82.3, 82.4; Fireworks Pixels 59.4; fizkes 112.1; flashpics 49.3; grafikplusfoto 114.9; Henry Czauderna 114.4; Hera, Jiri 76.3; imagesetc 114.6; industrieblick 114.7; irenegreco 36.2; JenkoAtaman 77.1; kite_rin 48.4; Kraskov, Veniamin 117.4; Lucky Dragon 41.5; majorosl66 40.6; McllittleStock 40.5; Monkey Business 59.9, 77.5; Monkey Business Images 114.3; monticellllo 41.4; nenetus 40.4; New Africa 49.2; Oleg 33.1; Ottoson, Jens 12.2; peterschreiber.media 111.6; phoenix021 67.5; photoschmidt 49.1; Pixelot 117.9; RossandHelen 77.7; Schmidt, Bernd 111.9; Schweitzer, Elena 83.4; serhiibobyk 114.8; Tosca M White 59.5; ValentinValkov 59.3; Vyshniakova, Diana 39.5; Wavebreak Media 117.2; womue 111.2; WONG SZE FEI 41.3, 41.6; ©jovannig 83.2. |Swati (Sanyal) Tarafdar, Vijayawada, Andhra Pradesh: 77.6. |Thinkstock, Sandyford/Dublin: Purestock 66.3; Siri Stafford 66.4. |Wefringhaus, Klaus, Braunschweig: 60.6.